WHY I STILL BELIEVE:
A JOURNEY INTO CHRISTIAN APOLOGETICS

BY JOSEPH BOOT
FOREWORD BY JAMES R. WHITE

 Ezra Press

Published by Ezra Press, a ministry of the
Ezra Institute for Contemporary Christianity
   PO Box 9, Stn. Main.
   Grimsby, ON
   L3M 1M0.

By Joseph Boot. Copyright of the author, 2021. All rights reserved. This book may not be reproduced, in whole or in part, without the written permission of the publishers.

Unless otherwise noted, Scripture quotations are taken from the New Living Translation. Copyright Tyndale Charitable Trust.

Scripture quotations followed by NKJV are taken from the New King James Version. Copyright Thomas Nelson Inc., 1982.

Study questions by Joseph Boot, Rachel Eras, Ryan Eras and Lauren Tamming
Cover design by Davie Peter and Rachel Eras
Interior design by Rachel Eras

For volume pricing please contact the Ezra Institute: info@ezrainstitute.ca

Why I Still Believe: A Journey into Christian Apologetics
ISBN: 978-1-989169-09-4

Dedicated to my parents Michael and Helen Boot,
Who faithfully sought to live by the scriptural command:
"Train up a child in the way he should go,
And when he is old he will not depart from it."
Proverbs 22:6 NKJV

TABLE OF CONTENTS

Foreword   vii

Intorduction to the Ezra Press Edition   xi

Introduction   19

1. By What Authority?   33

2. Covenant Child   53

3. School Dinners   63

4. Ridicule and Rebuttals!   77

5. Boot Camp   87

6. No Apology   93

7. The Heart of the Matter   105

8. Firm Foundations   137

9. A Matter of the Heart   155

10. The Robin and the Egg   173

Foreword

Giving a reasoned defense of the faith as a means of evangelizing the lost and edifying the saints has been the task of the church from the start. The Gospel is for all peoples, and it therefore must be taken into all the world. Yet the challenges that have faced the church across the world and across the centuries have varied greatly in their content and character. The initial conflict with Greek philosophies, or Gnostic mythology, formed the context in which apologists labored. In the Middle Ages in Europe an ostensible Christian consensus existed which focused attention upon theistic proofs. The Reformation took place within a culturally Christian context and, of course, most of its apologetic energy was dedicated to internal battles, that is, in reference to the claims of the Roman Catholic Church, the Papacy, gospel, etc. But it was not long until rationalistic thought began its march through the universities and out into the culture as well, and the modern age of skepticism, rationalism, and with the advent of Darwin, thoroughgoing naturalistic materialism, dawned.

The modern technological world presents a spectrum of challenges to the Christian faith that the early church surely would have found bewildering and challenging. Never before has there been as great a need for a consistent understanding of Christian truth, and how it needs to be presented to the world, than now.

The book in your hands is Joseph Boot's attempt to map out what a consistent approach to evangelism and a defense of the faith looks like in our modern day. Consistent in that Boot, along with an entire school of apologetic thought, believes that theology determines apologetics, not the other way around. That is, what you believe informs the content of the message you are seeking to communicate, and then delimits the methodologies you can consistently use to proclaim that message. You may come up with what look like some really effective arguments that "work," but if they are not consistent with the theology you are presenting, they are useless. Far too often Christians have gotten the proverbial cart before the proverbial horse and utilized apologetic methods that were not in harmony with the message they were supposed to communicate. The opponents of the faith are quick to detect such inconsistencies and throw them back upon those who are supposed to be representing truth itself.

The true value of this approach, as laid out here by Dr. Boot, is that it flows from the beautiful harmony that exists between divine truth and how the Apostles presented and defended it. For the modern believer, we can walk in their example, even as we face a much wider range of objections, as long as we understand and purposefully embrace the foundational truths they taught.

One of those truths is found in having a biblical view of man and God, rather than the confused perspective taught in so many churches today. One cannot "do" the work of presenting and defending the faith if one has a shallow or unbiblical view of man as the creature of God, made in His image, and yet living in consistent rebellion, suppressing the truth of God that has already been clearly revealed through what God has made (Romans 1:20-23). Man's spiritual standing, together with the reality of God's revelation in creation, render man "without excuse," or in other words, "without a consistent apologetic" (Romans 1:20). And though man may argue for his rebellion against God's revelation, he simply cannot do so *consistently* for he is living in God's world and having to borrow from God's ways to make his arguments. We are to point out his inconsistency and hence function as agents of the Spirit in bringing conviction to the heart.

Joseph Boot has practiced what he preaches in this book. As one of the leading cultural theologians and apologists in North America, Dr. Boot has spent years applying and tuning the concepts he lays out in this book in the public sphere. We are the welcome recipients of his wisdom and thought as we read his words in this book.

Prepare to be blessed, and at times challenged, by *Why I Still Believe*.

James R. White, November 2020

Intorduction to the Ezra Press Edition

From the Christian standpoint, the human person is by nature *homo respondens* (a responding being). This means that by virtue of creation we are made to *respond* to the Word of God in every aspect of our lives. Biblically, all of creation responds to the law-Word of God as His creature, but human beings are unique in their response-ability as His image-bearers. Another way of expressing this thought is that *all of life is religion* manifest in either a faithful and obedient or unbelieving and disobedient *response* to God. Consequently, a formative aspect of human experience is the *function* of belief or faith in which rests our sense of certitude. Every human being has a faith of some kind – a basic trust in something or someone, making belief an inescapable reality. Since no one is without belief in something that is given ultimacy and primacy as the origin or source of life and meaning, this book does not assume that the idea of 'belief' or 'faith' needs justification, as though some credulous humans have it and others don't. As Blaise Pascal pointed out, even if by force of habit, we all have to act upon some faith.

Rather this work intends to explain and defend why I *still* believe and trust as a man in the Creator and Redeemer I was taught to trust and put my faith in as a child.

Why I Still Believe was first published in 2005, which at the time of my writing this new introduction, is sixteen years ago – a reality hard for me to take in. I remember vividly the small study where I penned this work in our first family home in Canada, overlooking a colorful front garden – my eldest daughter being just three years old at the time. The years seem to have flown by as quickly as a leisurely game of cricket on a summer afternoon, reminding me of the words of Psalm 103:

> As for man, his days are like grass—
> he blooms like a flower of the field;
> when the wind passes over it, it vanishes,
> and its place is no longer known.
> But from eternity to eternity
> the Lord's faithful love is toward those who fear Him,
> and His righteousness toward the grandchildren
> of those who keep His covenant,
> who remember to observe His precepts.

Because of that faithful love, guaranteed in God's covenant, *I still believe* as fervently and passionately in the Christ of Scripture today as I did when I first sat down to write this book. Moreover, by God's generous grace that faith has grown and matured during the intervening years, granting me an ever-deepening insight into the goodness, power, and wisdom of Christ's restorative kingdom rule, which calls all creation back to a faithful response to His Word.

Of course, social history does not stand still as the time passes and over these years much has transpired in the cultural landscape regarding Christianity and the public space. For one, the 'New Atheists' were not household names when

Introduction to Ezra Edition

I wrote this book. For about a decade people like Richard Dawkins, Christopher Hitchens and Sam Harris rose swiftly in popular consciousness, repackaging some well-worn arguments against the God of Scripture in best-selling popular level books. Almost as quickly they seem to have faded from view as Hitchens passed away, the aging Dawkins became increasingly perceived as a ranting and comical caricature, and Harris revealed his essentially Buddhist faith in his mystical book *Waking Up*. Although I don't deal with these figures by name, the essential ground covered in *WISB* remains as relevant and applicable as ever in addressing the objections raised by the so-called new atheists.

In the second place, a ferocious assault on creational norms expressed in Scripture regarding human sexuality and identity has been unleashed at a terrifying pace in the last two decades. This was an emerging challenge that I touch on as a harbinger of persecution in the early part of the book. Shortly after *WISB* was published in 2005, same-sex 'marriage' was made law in Canada the same year. This decision opened the floodgates to judicial and cultural activism that has rapidly eroded what was left of biblical foundations and freedoms in our society to the point that this year Canada is on the brink of passing a Bill that would criminalize parents, pastors, therapists and counselors for advertising or providing help to minors dealing with unwanted same-sex attraction or gender dysphoria if that help was directed toward a faithful response to the scriptural norm for human identity and sexuality. Though I could not have predicted when writing the first edition that our culture would so quickly have been denying even the binary distinction of male and female in the law, the logic of this problem is anticipated as I deal with the problem of authority and in my discussion of foundational questions in chapter seven.

The essential form of argument I have used in the book is one that I still stand by and utilize sixteen years later. I am increasingly convinced that, to be persuasive in our cultural moment, this approach constitutes the necessary direction for a distinctly scriptural articulation and defense of the faith in a society that has lost touch with its foundations. In popular language we might call this method worldview apologetics, or cultural apologetics because it seeks to go to the religious root of people's beliefs, exploring the consequences and outcomes of those presuppositions and systems of thought for human life and knowledge.

In more formal or technical language, this approach to apologetics combines immanent and transcendental criticism. *Immanent* criticism places itself in the shoes of the opponent of Christianity and seeks to graciously highlight the inconsistencies and problems of intelligibility *within* non-Christian systems of thought. *Transcendental* criticism seeks to disclose the necessary *pre-conditions* of theoretical views of reality at their religious root and works to show that biblical Christian faith alone – in a satisfying and convincing way – provides adequate grounds for truth and knowledge, avoiding the hopeless contradictions and antinomies of non-Christian thought. In other words, this method tries to show that what is normative (i.e., laws and standards not *derived* from human thinking but *given* with creation to which we are all subject) is an inescapable and intrinsic part of human existence. As such, pretended autonomy (man as a law to himself) and a purely immanent explanation for reality (one that excludes the living God) are impossibilities. Perhaps an unusual feature of the book however is that these arguments are explained simply, in an introductory way and made more interesting and colorful by their interwovenness with an account of my own journey of thought and belief into my early thirties.

Unavoidably with passing years, maturation and growth, there are things in the book that I would now say somewhat differently, with greater depth and insight in places, with a change of emphasis here and there if I were writing a more comprehensively revised edition. In particular, my strong emphasis on the valid metaphor of *sight* for knowledge I would have moderated and expressed in light of the primary metaphor of *hearing* for a scriptural view of knowledge – a theme that emerges in the last two chapters and concludes the book. This is vital because creation is by the *Word* of God and salvation comes by *hearing* the Word. All people are called to listen to that Word and respond by believing in order to truly understand. As God the Father bore witness concerning His own Son, "This is my beloved Son. I take delight in Him. *Listen* to Him." (Matt. 17:5)

How to use this book

Apologetics has often been treated as a 'tool' or 'technique' in the service of evangelism, one that can be picked up or put down as the occasion requires. Whilst apologetics has an important role in our evangelistic witness, I believe this characterization of apologetics is mistaken. Posing the question, "When does a person need to use apologetics?" is often depicted as a question akin to "when should a person use a hammer?" I believe a better analogy is "when should a person use their hands?" For most of us, hammering is rarely required, but we use our hands almost every minute of every day. Christian apologetics is not primarily a technique or activity that is separate from ordinary Christian life; it is part and parcel of a larger Christian world-and-life-view. We will return to this concept in the following pages, but what it means at the outset is that my goal in this book is not to provide an apologetics 'handbook' in the sense of a list of top talking points, pre-wrapped answers or polished formulas for you to memorize; what I am interested in communicating is a fundamental way of thinking about the world, and all of our activities in it, and exploring apologetics as the vindication of a Christian vision for living in God's created order.

The Christian apologist must first and foremost be a person who sets apart Jesus Christ as Lord of their entire being and who seeks to bring their whole life (concentrated in the heart) into conformity with His Word and example (1 Pt. 3:15). The Christian world-and-life-view is deeper and more complex than a set of propositions, and my hope is that you would understand and internalize the apologetic approach set out here in terms of their place within a holistic and integral Christian response to the total Word of God.

One notable change that readers will find in this version compared to previous versions is the addition of study questions at the end of each chapter. Over the past few years I have been humbled and encouraged to learn that churches, Christian high schools, and homeschooling families have been using *Why I Still Believe* as a textbook for apologetics classes. Several teachers and parents suggested that I include some questions for discussion and reflection, and in some cases provided questions that had been particularly effective at sparking student responses.

In the work of apologetics, our aim is not simply to convince our conversation partner of the correctness or reasonableness of our viewpoint by multiplying evidence and arguments. Rather we seek to make clear the compelling beauty, authority and power of the gospel that it might capture hearts and minds. And this is most effectively done when, by stepping into their shoes for the sake of discussion, we prompt our interlocutor to examine and reflect upon their own assumptions and commitments and where they lead. We then invite them to consider human experience in light of the Word of God. It's the approach I commend in real life, and I have the same goal and focus with this book.

Accordingly, you will find that the study questions focus more on reflection than on recall. It is more valuable for the student to grapple with and master the ideas in this book than to simply repeat the arguments and statements as I have formulated them. A great question, it has been said, is a simple question with no simple answer. This is more work for the student, but is also much more rewarding, as they will be equipped to apply the principles of Christian apologetics and

Introduction to Ezra Edition

worldview to their own context and situation.

If parents or teachers decide to use the discussion questions as a basis for written assignments, the first couple of questions in each chapter can usually be answered more briefly, in a paragraph or two, while the later questions are more suitable to essay-length responses.

Joe Boot, February 2021

Introduction

This is a book I did not intend to write! Something about this fact gives me a greater sense of satisfaction than if I had planned the project for many months. I sat down at my desk to begin writing a lecture I was scheduled to deliver to a group of skeptics at a Canadian university. But I just kept writing! Four weeks later I had finished what I wanted to say.

This book is more personal to me than my previous work which is perhaps why it came with a good deal of ease; having said that, I do not claim that the ideas communicated in this book are original. In fact, I have often asked myself, as we all do, whether I have ever had an original thought. I think the answer to that question is no. When you have spent many years reading in a particular field, it is at times hard to know if a given thought you have is your own or not. The world has a long history of "thinking," and there is nothing new under the sun. I think I can safely say that the arguments presented here have been put in similar and diverse ways by various authors, probably more coherently than I have managed, but my story here is obviously my own and the arrangement of the material is what makes the same truths differ in emphasis, scope, and impact.

In a moment of excessive modesty one of my favorite Christian thinkers, Blaise Pascal (1623-1662) – referred to by Malcolm Muggeridge as "unquestionably one of the greatest intellects of Europe" – made this very point about his own work, disclaiming any originality, though I have never found his like. Pascal writes:

> In what I am writing, let no one think I am saying anything new. It is only the arrangement of my material that may be new. For it is like a game of tennis, where we both play with the same ball, but one of us uses it to better advantage. So I would like it to be said that I am simply using *well-worn words in a new framework. For when similar thoughts are rearranged, they simply present a different way of communicating the truth. So too, we can use our words.*[1]

For a number of years, I have greatly benefited in my life and work through reading Pascal. I also want to acknowledge a particular debt to the work of another Christian thinker, Cornelius Van Til, whose outstanding contribution to Christian philosophy has also shaped my approach to apologetics[2] and whose writings directly inspired me to write this little book. In fact, a considerable amount of the thought content of this book is simply a restatement and exposition of the fundamental truths that he and some of his students have addressed in decades past. Before I discuss him, I would first like to belie the possible impression that my book has the very limited scope of addressing only those familiar with, or interested in, the largely unnoticed field of Christian apologetics and some of its great thinkers. Such an impression would be the opposite

---

[1] Blaise Pascal, *Mind on Fire: A Faith for the Skeptical and Indifferent*, ed. James M. Houston (Bethany House Publishers, 1997), 47, emphasis mine.

[2] The field of Christian thought and activity that offers a rational vindication of the Christian philosophy of life through a reasoned defense and positive proof of the faith revealed in the Bible.

INTRODUCTION

of my intended objective. So please do not allow yourself to be put off by a few unfamiliar names and terms. The purpose of this introduction is to give some insight into my thinking as an author and what has shaped that thought, not to ostracize the reader. Intellectual honesty is very important in effective communication, and acknowledgement of debt in the area of your thinking serves good communication.

Approaching new areas of knowledge and fields of human culture can be intimidating. I remember well my sense of being an "outsider" when I first got to know some of my wife's friends. For years she had been involved in the performing arts, particularly ballet and physical theater. She had trained in a London ballet school and a London school of speech and drama. I, on the other hand, knew little about ballet or physical theater. As one of a family of six on a low income, we did not have the means to go to the ballet, opera, or theater. I recall only one visit to see a professional play whilst growing up. During my college years I had opportunity to see a little more, but still felt largely ignorant about this world of thespians and dancers. I felt isolated in the conversations and a little "uncultured." But soon I began to get a firmer grasp on what was being discussed and even began to be able to distinguish the excellent actors and dancers from the good ones, based on poise and technique. The "semi-technical" terminology began to become familiar and I saw many plays and musicals which I thoroughly enjoyed. Today there are few things I enjoy more than an opportunity to see a ballet, take in a classic musical, or get lost in a piece of theater.

What at first appeared a foreign and somewhat impenetrable world opened up to me as I broadened my horizons, resisting initial feelings of ignorance, and allowed my wife to lead me into a new realm of culture that had a great deal to offer. If we fail to engage with the unfamiliar because we feel ill-equipped or uninformed, we can never learn anything new. It is, then, my hope that those who are not even familiar with the basics of Christianity will enjoy and profit from this book and enter into, as it were, a new realm of discovery.

So then, in addition to Pascal, the other thinker that has deeply influenced my defense of Christianity is Cornelius Van Til (1895-1987). My first encounter with the work of this unique Christian philosopher was through reading a little-known lecture he wrote called "Why I believe in God." From then on, I was hooked and have been an avid reader of his work and the work of some of his noted students ever since.[3]

What most impressed me about both Pascal and Van Til was not simply their brilliant minds but their devotion to the authority, centrality, and indispensable nature of the Christian Scriptures in apologetics. The Bible is not relegated to the background, a source of embarrassment, seen as "hampering" the work (as appears to be the case with some modern apologetics), but rather as authoritative revelation supplying the principles and content that form the basis of our defense. The *proof*, both for Pascal and Van Til in their differing, but I think complementary, approaches to apologetics, was found *in* the revelation of God resting upon biblical criteria, not built upon philosophies outside of it!

Neither Pascal nor Van Til sought the proof for Christian theism outside the self-attesting Christ of Scripture, as though abstract principles of self-governing human reasoning are required to "approve" the possibility of God's revelation in Christ. Instead, they both sought to show that the only proof of God is found in the Christ of Scripture, Van Til showing that only upon this foundation can Christianity be effectively

---

3   For those familiar with the presuppositional approach to apologetics, my obvious debt to Cornelius Van Til will be very apparent throughout. In many respects this book is simply a personal exposition and exploration of presuppositional apologetics, based upon and reflecting the thinking of Van Til, and influenced as well by Greg Bahnsen and John Frame, two of Van Til's students. This personal exposition and application of Van Tillian and Pascalian thought is set in the context of my story and how I have come to understand my experience. I have employed certain terms that are largely unique to the presuppositional school.

Introduction

defended and be seen as the only possible foundation for knowledge and the intelligibility of human experience. It was their uniquely biblical approach, one focusing on the explanatory power of the biblical plotline accounting for the human predicament, and the other on epistemology[4] found in Scripture, that drew me to these authors, in whom I found wise guides in defending the truth of God's Word, whilst humbly *surrendering* to it. Apologetics can be a hazardous occupation, the constant temptation being to depend on human wisdom and learning the principles of this world rather than upon the Word of God.

In these two "guides," I believe I have found two faithful servants of God, among many in the long history of the Church, who like Augustine (AD 354-430)[5] and John Calvin (AD 1509-1564),[6] whose theology they both reflect (including Pascal in my opinion), are concerned above all else with the honor and glory of God. Thus, for Pascal, Christ is the "God of Abraham, God of Isaac, God of Jacob, not of philosophers and scholars."[7]

It was reflecting again on their work that inspired me to write my own account of why I still believe in Jesus Christ. One of Van Til's former students, the noted reformed theologian John Frame, records he was also deeply influenced by Van Til's approach to apologetics, and especially liked the short pamphlet *Why I believe in God*. John Frame expresses the conviction that this pamphlet sets an excellent example for Christian persuasion for those concerned with having a

---

4   Refers to one's theory of knowledge – its nature, source, and limits.

5   The most famous and influential of the Western church fathers, a philosopher and theologian of great significance who became Bishop of Hippo in northern Africa.

6   A brilliant and influential French theologian and reformer, along with Martin Luther the most important in Europe especially noted for his work in the Swiss city of Geneva, and his monumental *Institutes of the Christian Religion*!

7   Pascal, *Mind on Fire*, 41.

distinctly biblical approach and method. In his important work *Cornelius Van Til: An Analysis of His Thought,* Frame writes: "I believe that [*Why I Believe in God*] is, on the whole, an admirable *model* for Christian apologetics, in style, intellectual depth, comprehensiveness, conciseness, rapport with the reader, and biblical soundness."[8]

I am in broad agreement with these sentiments and have heeded his advice in the following account of my faith. My paternal Dutch heritage, Christian family background, and some other commonalities with Van Til's experience may have predisposed me to taking this view, but these "environmental factors" are obviously outside my control.

I have also sought at least to approach an appropriate comprehensiveness and depth, but I certainly do not suggest I possess the same penetration or clarity of mind as my guides. However you approach apologetics, you must argue with some model and structure in mind, particularly in terms of your epistemology, and here I am unashamedly of a "Van Tillian" shape.[9]

You might then ask whether it isn't somewhat inauthentic of me to argue *why I still believe* having based my work, broadly speaking, upon the structure of thought and epistemology of a particular Christian thinker and school of apologetics? In reply, I would claim that we all accept guides in our lives of some sort. There is nothing new under the sun; no human being can avoid thought-plagiarism; we are all products of our key influences. As Pascal himself rightly

---

8   John Frame, *Cornelius Van Til: An Analysis of His Thought* (Phillipsburg, NJ: P & R Publishing, 1995), 336.

9   The broad structure of my argument would be considered revelational presuppositionalism which is generally attributed to the fresh thinking of Van Til. In simple terms, it means that in apologetic argument and discourse you presuppose the truth of biblical revelation as the ultimate criterion for truth, as opposed to some other criterion found in the intellectual principles of non-Christian philosophy. You then proceed to show that knowledge, intelligible experience, or proof itself is impossible on any other foundation than the presupposition of the Scriptures which are self-attesting.

noted, when people speak about "their book" they often fail to acknowledge that there is much more of other people in it than there is of them! Van Til himself stood in the line of other Dutch thinkers, like Abraham Kuyper, and certainly believed he was merely developing, in the field of apologetics, the thought of the French reformer of Geneva, John Calvin. We all "adopt" one approach to reality or another. In the field of apologetics (whilst there is some overlap) many would identify themselves as "classical" in the Thomistic school of thought (following Thomas Aquinas), and not as presuppositionalists.[10] There are many other admirable guides in apologetics, like the brilliant C. S. Lewis who has inspired and been a model for numerous apologists.

It seems to me that when we reflect on our own life experience it takes a good deal of time to understand it properly, and we invariably need the help and insight of others in our quest for true understanding. Have I always viewed my past life in the way it is portrayed in this book? No, not exactly. We grow and change over the years and maturity helps us to understand ourselves and our experience better. For example, when I was growing up I tended to assume that my experience of church was definitive. The way we worshiped must be the right way. But as I matured I saw that other expressions and styles of Christian worship were also legitimate and could inform and enrich my own.

To illustrate it in another way that perhaps more can relate to, many people unconsciously view the marriage of their parents (if they grew up in a home with two married parents) as *the* model of marriage.[11] Later in their own marriages

10   It could be argued that most of the basic elements of presuppositional apologetics are found in the work of the church fathers Augustine and Tertullian as well as the eleventh-century Archbishop of Canterbury St Anselm, and the previously mentioned reformer John Calvin. All placed the necessity of a faith commitment as prior to true reason or understanding.

11   Marriage as defined by the Bible is between one man and one woman for life. It is seen as a picture of Christ's relationship with His Church. Sacrificial self-giving love is the Christian ideal for marriage.

they can take false expectations or fears into the relationship because they saw the marriage of their parents as normative. Again, as they mature, they see that it was one imperfect example of a marriage relationship that need not exhaust their understanding of what marriage actually should look like. In fact, sometimes we all need our misperceptions shaken to the core.

The actual experiences we have in life are what they are, but how we understand and interpret our experience (as children or churchgoers, for example) changes or develops. We often talk about the "gift of hindsight," and it is a gift, because as we look in retrospect at our lives many things we may have missed or misinterpreted before can take on vital new meaning and significance. We are able to see patterns more clearly and observe how one path has led into another.

Fairly recently, I was bemused when experiencing some significant knee pain while enjoying playing my favorite sport – soccer. When I told my friend, he suggested that both my distance running in my teens and my recent eating habits, with perhaps excessive sugar, may have contributed to this. Looking back, I could see that he may be right. Years of pounding the road and recent complacent neglect of a more "wholegrain" diet appeared suddenly as potential causes of my discomfort. Altering my diet seemed to have a significant effect within a matter of weeks. It took my friend to cajole me into reflecting retrospectively on my past to see how my present had been affected!

During the last few years, I have been able to reflect with greater insight and maturity on my past and so been able to interpret it better. As you come to know God, His Word, and thereby yourself better, life can be consistently re-examined in a fresh, or more accurately, greater light, and consequently new insights come to the fore. It is a bit like the difference between viewing a country landscape at dusk and then seeing it again at noon: the clarity of midday enables you to see a great deal of detail that was imperceptible at dusk the

Introduction

previous day. So, despite the fact that I have not always intentionally articulated my life experience with the biblical view of knowledge I found in the guides I have mentioned, this view was, as I reflect, always present intuitively (a view at dusk) and that is perhaps why, as time has moved on, I have come more "consciously" to see things in this way, in the greater light of noonday.

It is my conviction that the approach to apologetics in this book is in accord with the Bible and will consequently benefit those who read it. Biblical truth requires restatement for each generation in a way that they can understand and relate to. The guides I have spoken of have gone to be with the Lord Jesus Christ whom they served, some centuries ago, some just decades. They preached and argued for the truth with clarity and conviction for their generation. Standing on their shoulders, I want to take those same truths and restate them in as relevant and clear a manner as I am able. The truth does not change, neither do the principles by which we must come to understand the truth, but each generation needs those who will faithfully restate the faith of our fathers and "contend earnestly for the faith which was once for all delivered to the saints" (Jude 3 NKJV). I have sought to accomplish this by telling something of my story of faith in this book and I have accurately interpreted my experience to the best of my current knowledge and ability.

I should emphasize that my objective has not been to give a detailed account of my life story. I do not delve deeply into various personal circumstances and struggles to show how God has sustained, strengthened, and guided me at every point, in the highs and the lows. I have not set out to write a life testimony (I am far too young for one thing), taking the reader on an emotional rollercoaster. Neither have I sought to document a purely "spiritual journey," as such. There are many superb and exciting books available retelling the amazing stories and adventures of believers as they have achieved great things for God in the far-flung corners of the globe or overcome tragedy and loss, by the grace of God, people with life experiences far more engaging and captivating than my own.

That is not to say that my personal walk with Jesus Christ through the varied circumstances of my life thus far is not utterly central to my faith – not at all. Rather, as a matter of emphasis, I have sought to accomplish something different to which I am, perhaps, better suited to achieve. I have attempted to explore something of my personal history and experience, with a particular focus on my intellectual journey and growing convictions about the truth. Interwoven with this account, I seek to build a coherent argument for the truth of Christianity, showing *why I still believe* today, as a man, in the same Christ I was taught to believe in as a child. I have done this specifically to avoid a misleading impression that can, at times, be made upon the religious skeptic by "testimony" devoid of an argument, that Christianity is a purely subjective and emotional issue, an incommunicable experience of a given individual that is not accessible to public critique or verification. Faith, it is then assumed, is not a rational life of trust based upon certain knowledge, but an arbitrary and irrational leap into the darkness, resting on an emotional preference. Nothing could be further from the truth, so I have studiously sought to avoid this false impression.

No doubt in the years ahead, God will enable me to see much more of Himself and in so doing I will see more of myself as I continue to grow in Christ. There is nothing exhaustive about my argument and I am still on my journey as a child of God, holding my Father's hand. There is still much to see and learn along the way!

To some extent I have shown you my hand in this introduction. I hope my upfront openness will not prevent you but rather encourage you to continue reading. I have believed in Jesus Christ and known His presence in my life since I was a small child. So this book represents my testament as to why I *still* believe as a man, and I am grateful and indebted to all those, from my parents, siblings, wife and children, to my

INTRODUCTION

colleagues in apologetics, to theologians and thinkers, who have helped me understand the Word of God, my faith, and myself. It is my simple prayer that these "well-worn words in a new framework" will challenge, encourage, and bless you. For the skeptical reader who is possibly unaware of the names I have mentioned so far or the particular relevance of what I have said here, I pray that this book will encourage you to re-evaluate your view of life itself. For the Christian, I hope it will strengthen your faith and perhaps inspire you to look at the work of some of these great theologians, past and present who, I believe, have much to teach us all. If you are a reader particularly interested in the area of Christian apologetics, my hope is that you will consider examining the life and work of Pascal, Van Til, and those who stand in their line of thought.

So, whoever you may be reading this, whether you are familiar with the relatively unknown discipline of Christian apologetics or not, I sincerely pray that my account of belief will in some way enrich you as a believer or revolutionize your life as one still seeking the truth. I long that you too would share in God's gift of faith – for "in Your light we see light" (Psalm 36:9 NKJV).

Why I Still Believe

Define and explain these words and phrases:

1. Self-attesting
2. Presuppositional

Answer the following questions:

1. Why does Joe compare learning about apologetics to learning about ballet and theater? What is something else you could compare it to?
2. What was unique about the apologetic approach of Blaise Pascal and Cornelius Van Til?
3. Joe uses the examples of church worship, marriage, eating habits, and viewing a landscape at different times of day or night to illustrate the experience of reflecting on his own life and upbringing, and why he still believes in God. Is your own life experience similar to Joe's or different? Is there an example that more accurately reflects your experience or more closely illustrates why you believe or disbelieve in God?
4. What role does the Bible play in Joe's approach to apologetics? Why does he approach apologetics this way? Have you seen other apologists treat Scripture differently than this? Give an example. Which approach do you think is better? Why?

Chapter 1
By What Authority?

"Fear of the Lord is the beginning of knowledge . . . For the Lord grants wisdom! From his mouth come knowledge and understanding . . . For wisdom will enter your heart, and knowledge will fill you with joy."

Proverbs 1:7; 2:6, 10

"I believe in order that I may understand."

- St. Augustine

Running scared

In my mid-teen years I did a lot of long-distance running. One day while I was running in the countryside of south-west England, in my home county, a veritable maze of lanes and hedgerows, I became confused and got completely lost – I had been focusing on getting a fast time rather than on the signposts! Seeing an elderly couple gardening in front of their cottage I asked for some directions. They asked me two crucial questions, "*Where have you come from and where are you going?*" I told them, and they then instructed me how to get back. I later discovered I had gone about three miles out of my way!

At some point in our lives, most of us have been similarly confused by our surroundings, becoming lost and disoriented in the physical world. But there is another form of human disorientation more widespread, more serious, and indeed more frightening than being merely geographically muddled: we might call it spiritual disorientation. We find ourselves existentially baffled. These are moments in life when we feel strangely lost, isolated, even alienated from we know not what. We then ask those same crucial questions but in a more ultimate sense, "*Where have I come from and where am I going?*" Consequently, some thinkers have referred to human beings as "cosmic orphans," lost and looking for home.

This "alienation" often leads us on to consider deep questions. Most of us at some point or another have given some thought to these ultimate issues of life. We have asked ourselves whether there is a God and, if so, what is He like? You may have given some thought to who you really are and what the meaning and purpose of your life actually is. Perhaps you have considered the prospect of death and asked whether there is life afterward.

Thinking about life after death often leads to reflection on whether there will be a judgment by God. Such ultimate considerations cause us to ask about the very *foundation* of our thinking and our behavior. This foundation or framework, whether thought through or not, forms our "world view," our understanding of reality (the nature of our existence in this universe), or our *theory of reality*. It is crucial that we all give this matter real thought if we have any sense of responsibility. How do you "get at" reality? From what source does your knowledge and understanding stem as you seek to answer such far-reaching questions? To feign indifference to these matters is, in itself, a very specific approach to reality with significant consequences for our thinking and behavior.

King Solomon, in the book of Proverbs quoted at the beginning of this chapter, puts forward a view developed throughout the entire Bible, culminating in the person of Jesus Christ, that acknowledgment of and reverence for God as the Creator and Sustainer of the universe is the very foundation, or first step on the road, to true knowledge and wisdom. In fact, it is the contention of the Bible and thereby true Christianity that people can know nothing as it truly is (in its true light) without seeing all of reality in the light of the transcendent, triune God of creation. For the Christian, God stands behind everything; He is our basic presupposition.

However, I am sure you have noticed that many people do not build their lives upon this foundation, but in fact quite the opposite. This is true of many people in all walks of life. For example, there are many able scientists and philosophers on both sides of this divide but in our modern, secular times it is the voice of "skepticism" that is often heard the loudest. Popular Cambridge physicist Stephen Hawking, reflecting this skepticism, writes: "I do not demand that a [scientific] theory corresponds to reality, because I don't even know what [reality] is."[1]

Philosopher Michael Scriven, in a passage where he attempts to place the entire burden of proof upon the theist and goes on to compare belief in God to belief in Santa Claus, writes: "We need not have a proof that God does not exist in order to justify atheism. Atheism is obligatory in the

---

1   Stephen Hawking and Roger Penrose, *The Nature of Space and Time* (Princeton: University Press, 1996), 121.

absence of any evidence for God's existence."[2] And notorious atheist Norwood Russell Hanson declares that theism "is a doctrine for which there are . . . no good reasons whatsoever for concluding that it is true. . . God does not exist precisely because the reasons theists advance for supposing that he does are all poor reasons."[3] Consequently, for such thinkers, atheism "wins" by default despite their inability to disprove God's existence – the philosophers have spoken.

Or have they? Despite these confident assertions, history is littered with genius minds who were Christian theists. Today's North American philosophical society's largest sub-group consists of Christian theists. This should at least make us pause before we swallow the extreme claims of many secular thinkers, journalists, scientists, and media personalities without due thought. We must take great care here in these skeptical times, for many Western intellectuals, in the contradictory guise of "tolerance" and "multiculturalism," seek to impose their elitist views with a totalitarian force upon the rest of us.

For instance, try publicly voicing a Christian view of the sanctity of marriage, sexuality, or even life, and watch the steam and hostility rise. In a recent case in Sweden a local pastor was sentenced to a month in prison for voicing the biblical view of homosexual practice during a Sunday sermon. It seems the philosophical position of modern secularism may not be questioned without accusations of bigotry, hatred, and "intolerance," whilst its adherents themselves seek to impose their "meta-narrative" (world view) of ethical relativism, uncritical pluralism, and religious skepticism upon us all, insisting that they alone have access to the truth about reality. I believe it is vital that we responsibly examine (rather than swallow) the credibility and basis of these astonishing claims.

---

2   Michael Scriven, *Primary Philosophy* (New York: McGraw-Hill, 1966), 102.

3   N.R. Hanson, "What I Don't Believe," in *What I Don't Believe and Other Essays*, ed. S. Toulmin and H. Woolf (Dordrecht: D. Reidel Publishing Co., 1971), 312, 313.

By What Authority?

Bare proof and naked facts

In the light of all this, how do we navigate our way through the winding lanes of life and its confusing array of philosophical options? Lost and disoriented by these competing views of reality, what do we do? Is it simply a matter of sitting down with cold logic and finding right conclusions at the end of a syllogism?[4] The brilliant seventeenth-century scientist, philosopher and Christian persuader, Blaise Pascal points out in his *Pensées* that much of what we humans believe has less to do with rational "proof" and more to do with habit and environment (or custom) than most of us would like to admit:

> Indeed, how little we really do prove. For proofs only convince the mind. But habits provide us with more effective and widespread proofs, modifying the mind without ever being conscious of it. For example, how can we prove that we shall die, or that there will be a tomorrow? Yet what could be more obvious? It is habit that really tends to convince us, and indeed, it makes us either Christians, or even Turks, or pagans, or merchants, soldiers or anything else. In all of these we have to act upon *some faith* that lies beyond where "bare proof" will take us . . .[5]

Apart from pointing out the limits of the scientific method to prove anything (we shall come to this later), Pascal seems to be describing two factors that are common to all of us. First, the process of "normalization." As we grow up, we accept things as being true without a shred of "proof" all of the time, all on the basis of "authority" provided by the habit of our environment. For example: why is a cat a cat? A hat a hat? Why is anything

4   A syllogism is a logical argument classically developed by Aristotle in *Organon* (meaning "tool"), normally arranged in the form of a major and a minor premise and a conclusion. In a valid argument the conclusion should follow the premises. A sound argument is when the premises are true and the conclusion follows the premises!
5   Pascal, *Mind on Fire*, 46-47.

what we assume it is? We have no "proof" that these categories and analytical statements are legitimate. Why is a tree a tree? And what makes it a tree? After all, we identify trees by their leaves and branches, trunks and roots, but we identify these particulars by the fact that they belong to that object we call a tree – a circular process! Likewise, in terms of "pure" (or bare) reason and logic, we cannot *prove* that the sun will rise or that the universe was not created five minutes ago with our current memories pre-programmed, and the scientific method (empiricism) cannot prove it either, yet no one I have ever met believes such outlandish things.

So, all these descriptive "facts" (about hats, cats, trees, memory, time, space, etc.) we learn and believe to be true about reality on the basis of authority, via the custom and habit of our environment – not because someone has proved them to us. This is one of the things that makes us human. We all accept the authority of habit in one form or another. We all assume we are *subjects* who know there are *objects* to be known and we embrace *authoritative guides* (like parents and teachers) throughout our lives to help us know how to relate these objects to each other. These guides help us to bring logic and reason (our rational thought process) into "fruitful relationship" with the world of objects. I have two young daughters and they are both developing under parental guidance in this way every day: learning what objects are called and how they relate, counting, describing and defining, yet I offer them no proof. The constant reiteration of these "facts" leads to a habit of description until they unconsciously accept as true what I have said. Given that this process must be projected back through all human history we might well ask, what is the original source of this incalculable wealth of knowledge and pre-programmed language hardware, proffered without an independent proof of its legitimacy?

Secondly, I think Pascal identifies what we can call basic "presuppositions." There is no proposition without presupposition. In other words, in making any statement about reality we bring a network of assumptions or beliefs (some faith) that underlie our statement. For example, if a scientist says, "It seems there may have been liquid water on Mars," he is affirming a certain set of beliefs. He "believes" (takes for granted) that there is a real objective universe out there that is so correlated to his mind that true knowledge can arise. He believes that "facts" are there to be discovered and his logical, rational process is valid in exploring these "facts." His mind, he assumes, is giving him reliable information and his senses are not deceiving him.

Albert Einstein once said, "The most incomprehensible thing about the universe is that the universe is comprehensible." Although fascinated by Jesus, Einstein rejected the personal, absolute God of the Bible. This led naturally to his bemusement that the universe appears comprehensible to us. The same bewildering problem is common to many modern scientists who hold naturalistic[6] beliefs, for to them the universe is "just there," a chaos of contingency – matter in motion! On serious reflection they are forced to ask how *ultimate chance* could possibly be intelligible to us. Einstein (like many philosophers of science today) was admitting that he could not "justify" or account for the intelligibility (comprehensibility) of the universe based on his own presuppositions[7] about it. Yet in order to do science, all scientists must take this intelligibility for granted. So Pascal rightly points out: "in all of these we have to act upon some *faith* [pre-commitment] that lies *beyond* where *bare proof* will take us" (my emphasis).

What this means is that even before we talk about "facts" and "proof" we must ask what our criteria for proof are and what our philosophy of fact is, for these lie beyond

---

6   Naturalism is the world view which holds that all reality is made up of matter and energy in motion ultimately subject to random chance. They believe there is no absolute unity in the chaos.

7   Presuppositions, as I use the term here, are a network of beliefs or foundational assumptions that add up to form a world view, through which we interpret reality, and by which we rate the plausibility of a given hypothesis.

or prior to our "proofs" and we naturally receive these criteria on the basis of *authority – on faith*. The pertinent questions for us are: which authorities have we listened to, why have we embraced their principles, and do they annihilate meaning and the intelligibility of experience, or provide a basis for it?

Bang out of order – explosive assumptions

Every fact, to be a fact, must be interpreted according to a framework or world view with given criteria for proof and a set of philosophical assumptions – there are no uninterpreted facts! A helpful illustration of this can be gleaned from the scientific community and the discussion among cosmologists about the origin of the universe. Most of us will have heard of the big bang hypothesis, but many would be unaware that a lot of physicists and cosmologists do not accept this "story of the world" as true and are looking at other models (interpretations) to explain the existence and phenomena of the universe. Consider the following statement from a recent article in the noted *New Scientist* journal, a statement co-signed by more than thirty highly qualified scientists from ten countries:

> Big bang theory relies on a growing number of *hypothetical entities* – things that we have *never observed*. Inflation, dark matter and dark energy are the most prominent. Without them there would be *fatal contradictions* between the observations made by astronomers and the predictions of the big bang theory. In no other field of physics would this continual recourse to new *hypothetical objects* be accepted as a way of bridging the gap between theory and observation. But the big bang theory cannot survive without these fudge factors . . . the successes claimed by the theory's supporters consist of its ability to retrospectively fit observations with a steadily increasing array of adjustable parameters, just as the old Earth-centered cosmology of Ptolemy needed layer upon layer of epicycles.

By What Authority?

> Yet the big bang theory is *not the only framework available for understanding the history of the universe* . . . other alternative approaches can also explain the basic phenomena of the cosmos . . . in cosmology today doubt and dissent are not tolerated, and young scientists learn to stay silent if they have something negative to say about the standard big bang model. Those who doubt the big bang model fear that saying so will cost them their funding. *Even observations are now interpreted through this biased filter, judged right or wrong depending on whether or not they support the big bang.*[8]

We see here, then, the practical impossibility of neutrality in our thinking illustrated for us in the one discipline so often considered "neutral," natural science. Every theory in science involves a "pre-commitment" of sorts and is always "framework" dependent. To put it another way, it is well known to philosophers of science today that all "evidence" in science is theory laden. That is, to be evidence at all it has already been interpreted in the light of a theory! Scientists themselves are hopelessly biased: they cannot help it.

You Were Just Brought Up That Way!

I have made these observations and comments concerning proof and authority at the beginning in order to "level the playing field" and defuse the most common rebuttal thrown at me as a young student, "You only believe that because your parents taught you to believe; you were just brought up that way!" I reject this charge for reasons I will give later. However, I do not deny that I was taught to believe in the triune God of the Bible. I used to believe that coming from a committed Christian family weakened my apologetic considerably; I have grown to think otherwise.

---

8   Eric Lerner, "Bucking the Big Bang," in *New Scientist*, 22 May 2004, 20 (my emphasis).

Why I Still Believe

You may now be feeling a little suspicious of my developing argument, and understandably so. Most of us have been led to believe that if someone is brought up in a religious tradition, their convictions should automatically be considered suspect, ruled out as the result of environmental conditioning alone. But this judgment should always be reserved if we want to reason in a fair or sound way. It is an informal logical fallacy to rest a conclusion purely on an appeal to someone's history and background. To illustrate, should a Conservative politician be deemed "unreliable" or as having "dubious" convictions and thereby excluded from running for party leadership, purely because his or her father was a famous Conservative leader? One would hope not! Such individuals should be judged on the basis of the legitimacy and coherence of *their* current views, policies, and leadership ability, not pre-judged as somehow "thoughtlessly right of center" because of the Conservative environment they grew up in. Their apparent Conservative convictions should be tested on their own merits. Likewise, my belief as a Christian should not be viewed with suspicion simply because I grew up in a Christian environment.

I hope to show that my early life as a child, accepting a particular authority, is consistent with my life today as a man. I assert (as opposed to "argue" at this point) that the God of the Bible was the guiding hand and constant presence in my early life, by whose providence my life has been subsequently directed, and because of whom my life and existence in this marvelous universe is made comprehensible and meaningful to me. As Cornelius Van Til explains: "Now in fact, I feel that the whole of history and civilization would be unintelligible to me if it were not for my belief in God. So true is this, that I propose to argue that unless God is back of everything, you cannot find meaning in anything."[9]

This is the line my apologetic argument seeks to take, and in a recent live radio discussion I sought to outline this ap-

---

9   Cornelius Van Til, "Why I believe in God," from *The Works of Cornelius Van Til* – 1895-1987, ed. Eric Sigward (CD-ROM version, published by Labels Army Co.).

proach with a philosophy professor from a Canadian university. During the debate a Ph.D. student of philosophy suggested that if I had grown up in Pakistan (as an illustrative instance of her point) I would not have believed in Jesus Christ as the Son of God and the Bible as God's authoritative revelation to humankind. Again, this is an understandable (though muddled) position to take, expressing the popular idea that truth is subjective[10] because of our unique individual conditioning. She intended to imply that I am only a Christian because I grew up in a so-called "Christian country" and was taught to believe. It is true that you can think merely in terms of "probabilities" and ask how many people born in Pakistan are Christians who believe the Bible? Noting they are relatively few, given the population size, it is typical to suppose you are offering some valid "support" for the idea of subjectivism.

But the student has merely begged the question. In making her assertions about my belief in Christ she has already *assumed* that the God of the Bible who created and sustains the whole universe, making His truth known everywhere and governing the course of history in His providence, does not exist. She has assumed that the events of history and the locations of people are essentially random.

If the God of the Bible does not exist, then in terms of mathematical probability my belief in Jesus Christ, on the basis of being born and raised in Pakistan, would be improbable (although probability has no meaning in a Godless universe, as we shall see). But she did not establish that Jesus Christ is not the eternal God as claimed in Scripture who in sovereignty appoints the place of our birth. Her emotive point was a fairly typical example of faulty reasoning, the kind we hear so much of in popular culture, particularly concerning God, Christians, and Christianity. Her line of argument was essentially *irrelevant prejudicial conjecture and hasty generalization,* bearing no

---

10   Not public and objective but an autobiographical quality – a psychological confidence particular to the individual that is not open to inspection from the outside. On this basis, the invalidity or validity of a given belief cannot be adequately assessed.

relevance to the issue in question, the truth or falsehood of the claims of Christ and thereby the legitimacy of my belief. We should avoid these sorts of rabbit trails and speculations and focus on the question in hand – the truthfulness of Christ and His Word.

NOT BY ACCIDENT

By God's providence, I believe, I was born in Greater London, England, and grew up for the most part in the small obscure country town of Devizes in the heart of Wiltshire, a largely agricultural county in southwest England. My paternal heritage is Dutch, as indicated by my surname, which simply means "boat." My father is the son of a Dutch soldier who spent years as a bodyguard for the queen of the Netherlands and later joined the French Foreign Legion, doing foreign governments' dirty work. Before his conversion in his sixties, he was a man about as far from Christian morality as you can get. At the commencement of the Second World War, during some early skirmishes with the enemy in Europe, he was seriously wounded. After his recovery he left the Legion and joined the Dutch navy for the remainder of the war, stationed in England; it was here that he met my grandmother.

My mother grew up in Kent, England, with a middle-class atheistic father (prior to his conversion in his eighties) and, in her early twenties, found herself in search of "enlightenment" during the Sixties on the hippie trail in India, having completed her university education. Both of my parents were converted to Christ prior to the conversion of their parents and so did not grow up in homes where the Bible was read or taught. Both of them became Christians in unlikely circumstances, with interesting stories to tell. They later met at a Bible training school in England and married soon after in London. I was born, the third of five boys, in the early 1970s.

Perhaps you believe in mere fate or the "accident of birth;" I do not. Perhaps you believe in chance. I believe in

By What Authority?

God's providence and sovereignty. You perhaps believe, as Jean-Paul Sartre put it, that you are "ooze, oozing from ooze and going back to ooze;" I do not! I find myself unable to accept that something comes from nothing or that life is undirected and without teleological significance.[11]

So I was born, I believe by design, into the family of an anglicized Dutchman who later became a country pastor and then missionary to the Indian subcontinent. I grew up in "England's green and pleasant land," in the shade of Wiltshire's idyllic meadows and rolling countryside. What about you? Into what situation and family were you born? Were you not predisposed, by your circumstances, to believe anything?

If you are living in the Western world it is likely that you have been, to some degree, exposed to the Christian world view. You are possibly familiar with the concept of the God of Christianity, the triune God of the Bible, Father, Son, and Holy Spirit. You may be familiar with the basic beliefs of the Christian creeds and be conscious of the historic figure Jesus Christ, who was crucified by the Roman procurator Pontius Pilate, and was raised to life again, according to the apostles and early witnesses. On the other hand, none of this may be familiar to you, in which case Christianity as a whole will be largely unknown.

You may or may not believe in the God of the Bible I am describing, one who reveals Himself in Jesus Christ and the Scriptures. Perhaps like many other people you have not given the matter much thought or have had no opportunity to really consider the Bible's message – as a consequence you are not sure what you believe. But my story begins and ends with the God of the Scriptures. It is this God who is the focus of this book. I have come to the conclusion that it is pointless to talk about God, without knowing what kind of being one is talking about. Like my guides I do not want to argue merely that a higher being of some sort exists, but rather that

---

11 Does life have an overarching reason or purpose? The teleology of something concerns its overall purpose or the end in view. Is there a grand plan or grand design with a specific goal in mind?

God, if anyone is to believe in Him, *must be* the God of the Bible. In other words, I believe that there is no other rational contender for the title than the triune God revealed in Jesus Christ. In my philosophy classes at school we described Him, by no means exhaustively, as *"p.h.i.l.c.o.g."* Each letter represented one of His characteristics, "perfect, holy, infinite, loving, creator, one, and good." *What* kind of God exists is inseparable from the question asking *whether* God exists. We cannot answer the latter without tackling the former. The God of Christianity will, then, be the basis of this book for reasons that I hope will become increasingly clear.

The Problem of Perspective

Allow me to express what I hope will be your approach to my little book and also hazard a guess at what you might be anticipating in the following pages. My hope, of course, is that you will read and consider carefully what I am saying. On your part, I would imagine (rightly or wrongly) you are waiting to see if I can make it rational, tenable, and reasonable *to you* to believe in Jesus Christ as the eternal Word of God and the Father who sent Him. I am sure you would agree that certain expectations in this regard are unreasonable. I cannot, for instance, "prove my case," as some philosophers have demanded, by peeling back the sky to reveal a Zeus-like figure watching all the proceedings. No one can wheel in a mobile laboratory equipped with test tubes and gas burners ready to demonstrate that the substratum of the universe is upheld by God's being. I cannot formulate a mathematical equation for you that will end all disputes. If I could do any of these things, He would not be "p.h.i.l.c.o.g.," the God of the Bible and of the Lord Jesus Christ.

Without wishing to presume what you the reader are thinking, some of us tend to be somewhat more fair-minded than certain inflammatory philosophers and consequently I suspect you are not demanding such a pyrotechnical demonstration? Instead, in as "objective" and "dispassionate" a posture as possible, you are simply waiting to be convinced, by my logical arguments and abstract philosophical principles, that my belief is more than what you suspect it might be: psychological conditioning, subjective epiphany, irrational delusion, evolutionary phenomenon, or an emotional crutch to give me the aid I need in life due to my intellectual and mental frailty – forgive me if this sounds presumptuous, but all of these "explanations" have been suggested to me on numerous occasions during my life.

Can I offer the sort of convincing rational proof you may be seeking on the typical terms laid out above? There was a time, even as a Christian apologist, when I would have affirmed that if you would just be objective, setting aside your bias as we discuss Christianity, I could show you the great probability of its truthfulness. But I have since seen that I was always overreaching myself. I usually neglected to acknowledge to my questioners that I had a pre-commitment, and I also neglected to point out theirs. But I will not make that mistake now. I have faith in Jesus Christ as the Creator and Savior of the world. I cannot escape this reality or dodge it. I find myself unable to make sense of this world in any other light. If you do not share this pre-commitment, then whether you have intentionally thought it through or not, in principle (though perhaps not in your heart), you do not see yourself as a creature of the God of the Bible; your alternate *world view* rules this out. Consequently, I cannot presume that I can prove *to you* that the triune God should be believed – our understanding of facts is very different. I can only hope to show that it is reasonable *for you* to believe in Christ. This is a very important distinction.

I have a friend who is color blind. It is a fairly common condition. Such a person finds it difficult if not impossible to distinguish colors and see them for what they are. For the sake of argument let us agree that those who see in full color see properly, or with true perception, and those who don't, do not. I cannot prove to my friend that the sky is blue, that the grass is green, or that the sunset is red and golden; his cognitive position precludes it, he does not see color. Such people find themselves, with respect to the world, in an *epistemic position* where color distinctions can never be proved *to* them. They are predisposed to be blind to color.

The word "epistemology" concerns how we gain knowledge and "get at" reality. We all have an "intellectual attitude" toward ourselves, God, and the world we live in that is directly related to our epistemic position or perspective – our theory of reality. Because of this necessarily limited position, it is possible for things to be obscure or even imperceptible to us.

If I put on my wife's glasses, my perception is so altered that I would be considered seriously visually impaired, but for my wife these lenses correct her misperception of the world – when she puts them on, suddenly everything becomes clear. The proof, for my wife, that the world is not really as she perceives it to be *unaided*, comes when her "cognitive position" is altered visually, the glasses are on and things become clear.

As Pascal astutely observes in his *Pensées:*

> Whenever we want to be helpful in convincing someone that he is wrong, and so correct him, we also have to see things from his point of view. For perhaps he is right as he sees it, but he may also need to see things from a differing point of view. Perhaps it is in the nature of things that we humans can never see things from every possible angle and so we cannot see things completely. But this should not upset us, if we realize that this lies behind all wise correction.[12]

Thus, I do not intend to insult or offend you by implying your sight is impaired and that you need to look at things radically differently. I admit I want to show that you are tragically mistaken if you reject Jesus Christ as God, revealed in the Scriptures. At the same time I recognize that if you don't

---

12 Pascal, *Mind on Fire*, 46.

believe in Him, it is because of the way you are looking at the whole matter, not because you are the intellectual inferior of Christians. It is our point of view that determines what we see, and our point of view is controlled by our presuppositions. My attempt to correct you, then, is not out of arrogance or intellectual pride. As a Christian I know that *I cannot see things completely (every possible angle),* rather I recognize that only God sees all exhaustively. He alone is therefore able to correct people *authoritatively* and enable us to know who and what we are, and what this world is. Thus, it is on the basis of His authority that I offer a correction, not my own. This is the very basis of the Christian idea of revelation – the God-inspired Scriptures contain our ultimate criteria for truth. I contend that without this authoritative revelation from God who knows and sees all exhaustively, we humans could know nothing as it really is (in its true context). Ultimately, we would be lost and adrift in a world of foolish hypotheses, never in possession of all the facts. But because God has spoken we can know things are absolutely true, without knowing all facts exhaustively.

    I wish that I could lend my color-blind friend my eyes for a day so that his cognitive and epistemic position could change, and I could prove *to* him that the world is full of color. In talking with my friend about color, he must consider what I say just "for argument's sake," as he cannot "see" it himself, so that I can show him it is reasonable for him to believe the world is in color. As it happens, you might expect, my friend does believe strongly that the world is in color, even though he cannot see it with his physical eyes as I describe it. In order to accept this, he must not only change his belief about the world, he must change his belief about himself – this is much harder! He must concede that he does not see things completely as they are, he must accept that the problem is not out there with the evidence, but in himself, with his eyes and his brain's interpretation of the information. It is hard to change our beliefs about the world and even harder to change our beliefs about ourselves.

This, however, is precisely what is necessary when it comes to the question of God and the Savior Jesus Christ – this is a radical and seismic shift. Unfortunately, many people will not even entertain this as a possibility. So I cannot make it reasonable *to* you to believe what you do not want to believe or are predisposed not to believe given your point of view. No amount of evidence can prove *to* such a person what they cannot see or will not see by definition; the evidence will always be misinterpreted through color-blind eyes or the wrong spectacles that we have willfully glued to our faces. I can only hope to show you that it is reasonable *for* you to believe, and invite you to follow my argument for argument's sake, and so to alter for a time, at least intellectually, your epistemic position by looking at the "other side," from Pascal's "other perspective," and see if your vision is not corrected and things become clear as you put on the new lenses.

BY WHAT AUTHORITY?

DEFINE AND EXPLAIN THESE WORDS AND PHRASES:

1. Worldview
2. Presupposition
3. Proof

ANSWER THE FOLLOWING QUESTIONS:

1. Can you think of some things you believe simply based on authority or without proof? Why does this matter for all the things we believe? (p. 38)
2. How would you explain your own worldview? How did you learn it?
3. Have you ever been told "you only believe that because your parents taught you that"? How would you respond to this?
4. Why is it important to distinguish the God of the Bible from a generic sort of higher being? Joe was taught at school to think of God in terms of His characteristics: PHILCOG. How would you briefly define each of these characteristics? Are there any you would add or change if you were asked to describe God?

Chapter 2
Covenant Child

"You have taught children and infants to give you praise..."

Matthew 21:16

"Fellowship with Christ is communicated to infants in a peculiar way. They have the right of adoption in the covenant, by which they come into communion with Christ."

-John Calvin

Through the Eyes of a Child

I remember wanting to be like my father when I was a child. I recall on several occasions assembling in the family room a small congregation consisting of my three brothers and a couple of friends whom I had gathered to take in my sermonic efforts! I administered the Eucharist with fruit juice and cookies, if memory serves me correctly. Although these were effectively games, I was not gaming in the sense that I was mocking. On the contrary, I was persuaded from early in childhood that the Bible was true, to be believed and acted upon. I sensed its reality and importance despite my limited understanding. In fact, I cannot remember a time when I did not believe in Christ as Creator and Redeemer of the world.

I remember one day a video was being played in my home for members of the church my parents led. I was present watching the pre-recorded sermon. The American preacher was speaking about the importance of knowing Christ because He would return again to judge the world and only those who had received Him as Savior and Lord would be saved on that perilous yet wonderful last day. I recall going out on my bike after this, riding down toward the local canal and praying that God would save and forgive me and include me, a sinful individual, in His family – I prayed this over and over. This is just one of many similar instances in my early childhood. I sought to make sure on several occasions that God knew I wanted Jesus Christ as my Lord.

A few years earlier at about the age of eight, I was playing down at the local park with one of my brothers and several friends. I was the youngest there and the older children were playing a rather risky game. They were running across the top of a fifteen-foot-high brick shelter, then leaping across an iron fence to the grass bank on the other side. You needed speed and long legs. At eight years of age, these were qualities I was lacking! Nevertheless, I wanted to try as the reward (if I remember correctly) for this stunt was a kiss from a pretty girl in our school who was standing nearby awarding the jubilant young athletes their prize. I made my way up the brick edge of this flat-roofed building, as I was a good climber, and then surveyed the leap. How far away the grass bank looked to my eyes and felt to my legs. I watched an older boy make the leap; I looked again. I'll never make it, I thought to myself. The prospect of collecting my kiss lying down below in a heap with two broken legs was not appealing. One of the kids urged me to climb back down; I needed little encouragement. I began my descent but got my jacket caught at the top of a pole I was seeking to slide down. In trying to lift myself free, I fell fifteen feet and smashed my head on the ground, and apparently there I lay, largely unconscious (I can remember small bits), until a massive ambulance man – at least that's how he appeared to me – scooped me up and took me to hospital where I regained consciousness with my parents in the room.

It was thought at first that I had a fractured skull, was potentially going to lose sight in one eye, and had a suspected broken nose – it was not pretty. My parents went home and prayed with our church. Two days later I was released from hospital with no eye damage, a nose intact, and no fractures to the skull. I am all too aware of what many would say about my recovery: it was remarkably quick and surprising, but these things happen – I was fortunate, lucky, I beat the odds, and so forth. Nonetheless, I believe it was more than that. My family believed that it was God's grace. I had no idea until much later on that my parents and church family had prayed, and I was too young and ignorant to be a recipient of the "placebo effect" of prayer.

I tell these stories only to make clear the kind of atmosphere I grew up in. It was certainly an atmosphere where I was groomed in a particular direction. We were not in any sense a "wacky" religious family. Ours was not like the home of the infamous Christian Ned Flanders of the popular television series *The Simpsons*. My father's Dutch and military-style upbringing made him something of a disciplinarian in terms of structure and order to life. Things were not easy. I was by no means a spoiled child, nor was I over-protected and sheltered from the world. We were reliant upon the goodwill of other Christians given that we had such a large family and low income. Parcels of food would mysteriously arrive at our door. Checks would come through the post to pay for a family holiday, clothes would be handed down to us from other families – I can only remember one pair of new jeans being bought for me. Yet I do not recall feeling resentful about these circumstances. I rarely felt hard done by or mistreated, for I was conditioned to orient my life around God's will, not how many new things I could acquire; that is not to say I never desired new things. However, we were encouraged to make use of our time and possessions creatively and for God, seeking to be content with what we had. Consequently, I really enjoyed childhood, even though some of my friends found it incredible that we had no television till I was about eleven years old.

My father worked round the clock on two jobs from 5 a.m. till 11 p.m. as a postman and as pastor of a local country church because the income from our congregation was too small to support the family. He could be heard praying each morning. He would usually pray before going out on the morning delivery. Occasionally on a weekend at 6 a.m. I would go downstairs and sit in a chair near my dad while he prayed, and I would read my Bible. At all mealtimes we would pray and thank God for our food. We had a comical poster on the wall by our old oak kitchen table where we ate together. It depicted a large family round the dining table returning thanks for their tiny portions of food saying, "Heavenly Father, bless us and keep us all alive, there's ten of us for dinner and not enough for five." But we never went without.

Each morning, before we left for school, my mother, who was more refined and middle-class but no less hard-working and industrious than my father, would read from the Bible and pray with us, and we would pray for family, grandparents, friends, and fellow students, often that they would come to know Christ as their Lord and Savior. Twice a week we would spend time together as a family; we called them "family evenings." Part of those evenings invariably involved Dad leading us in family prayers and devotions. We would read from portions all over the Bible and were taught the story of Scripture: creation, humanity's fall from paradise as our first parents, Adam and Eve, disobeyed in the garden of God, and God's plan of rescue culminating in the life, death, and resurrection of Christ. We were taught to accept the Bible as the Word of God and that faith in Christ was a gift from God not to be squandered.

I am glad to say that in my parents' lives, what was preached was also practiced and therefore I grew up seeing a consistency between what was taught and how we lived. I was taught, or groomed, you might say, to believe the Bible's account of all of life and history in its entirety and in Jesus Christ whom the Scriptures reveal. This was never presented to us as a merely academic matter. My experience of Christianity as a child was not simply believing a set of propositions as true and leaving it at that. Rather, biblical faith was a reality that affected all the aspects of my life. I would often pray and read the Bible alone, persuaded by an inward conviction of the truth of Scripture, convince that I experienced no less than a real relationship with God, by the presence of the Holy Spirit.

Doubtless your upbringing was not so mystical, backward, or restrictive! I can hear your sympathy for me, a poor indoctrinated soul. How heartless to teach a child such draconian nonsense in this day and age. Conversely, your parents were modern and sophisticated, as they read from the *Humanist Manifesto II* or Darwin's *Descent of Man,* the secular scriptures of the world! You were not instructed in the ancient beliefs and ethics of a Semitic culture or taught "irrelevant" stories concerning 2,000-year-old incidents in Palestine regarding the poor carpenter from Nazareth. Your upbringing was defined instead by an enlightened open-mindedness and your growth not stunted by archaic religious dogmas. The choice was yours, of course; if you should end up interested in that "religious stuff" you could make up your own mind in later life.

Am I being sarcastic? Well, perhaps a little, because I am afraid this is the popular myth we nurture. As Van Til maintains:

> Shall we say then that in my early life I was conditioned to believe in God, while you were left free to your own judgment as you pleased? But this will hardly do. You know as well as I that every child is conditioned by its environment. You were as thoroughly conditioned not to believe in God as I was to believe in God. So let us not call each other names. If you want to say that belief was poured down my throat, I shall retort by saying that unbelief was poured down your throat.[1]

We have all been affected by our essentially religious environment, and a lack of teaching from our parents on moral issues, for example, is itself a very powerful form of instruction. Not to be in Christ is, by definition, to be against Him: there is no neutral territory! Indifference is a religious (metaphysical) position as much as atheism and skepticism are religious positions. It is obviously true that not to teach children about the God of the Bible and affirm that He is central and foundational to our understanding of everything is to affirm that He is not the ultimate criterion for truth and that the Christ of Scripture is not who He claims to be, "the way, the truth, and the life" (John 14:6).

So then, like your childhood, my early life was shaped, orientated, and aimed in a particular direction. As an infant I was dedicated to Christ by my parents who committed themselves to bringing me up with an understanding of the faith in a home in which I would be given every encouragement to embrace Christ as the Lord of the universe. At twelve years of age I chose to be baptized and publicly confess my own faith

---

1   Van Til, "Why I believe in God."

in Christ. Above my study desk I still have a picture of myself standing in the water that day decades ago. This began a crucial period in my life during which I slowly started to gain a greater understanding of God's plan, providence, and control over the course of history, giving me the wider context to understand what salvation in Christ actually meant for me and for this world.

To be a Christian is to recognize that we are image-bearers of God, made to think His thoughts after Him, to worship Him, and direct our lives toward obedience to Him in every field of human endeavor. In the context of space-time history, in the real world, not that of myth or make-believe, our first parents had disobeyed God, breaking covenant and rebelling against Him, involving all humankind in their rebellion. And we, continuing that rebellion in our own lives, need redemption (to be bought back from sin and Satan), salvation (rescue), and deliverance from the wrath of God. This is the story of Scripture, the outworking of God's plan of salvation – those who believe His promises and trust Him are considered covenant keepers. God in His boundless love sends His Son into the world to reveal to us the *"image of the invisible God"* (Colossians 1:15) and so fulfill His glorious plan of reconciliation, the covenant promise of grace and forgiveness. As the Scriptures say:

> Long ago God spoke many times and in many ways to our ancestors through the prophets. But now in these final days, he has spoken to us through his Son. God promised everything to the Son as an inheritance, and through the Son he made the universe and everything in it. The Son reflects God's own glory, and everything about him represents God exactly. [Christ] sustains the universe by the mighty power of his command. After he died to cleanse us from the stain of sin, he sat down in the place of honor at the right hand of the majestic God of heaven. (Hebrews 1:1-3)

That plan is all-encompassing as sin; it is not just personal but structural to the cosmos in its effects – the world is fallen! Human beings, as the instrumental cause of this catastrophe, are rebels against God who need to "throw down their arms," as C. S. Lewis once put it.

Thus, each of us, according to Scripture, is either a covenant (contract) keeper or covenant breaker as we inescapably stand in relationship to this God. The Bible teaches us there is no third position of neutrality. So, the great antithesis was clearly before me from an early age. On the one hand, there was the thinking and way of the world, and on the other, there was the way of love of God – thinking and living in submission to Him, for His glory, resulting in our highest happiness. As a result, I understand my childhood as being defined by the keeping of God's covenant (agreement), living as a blessed recipient of covenant promises. I was born into a family of covenant keepers and I have always regarded this as a marvelous privilege.

School Dinners

DEFINE AND EXPLAIN THESE WORDS AND PHRASES:

1. Covenant

ANSWER THE FOLLOWING QUESTIONS:

1. Joe quotes Cornelius Van Til, who says that "every child is conditioned by its environment. You were as thoroughly conditioned not to believe in God as I was to believe in God." Is this a fair statement? Why or why not?
2. What does it mean to say that each of us is either a covenant keeper or covenant breaker?
3. Have you ever thought of yourself as a rebel against God? Does that change the way you think about God, ourselves, or the task of apologetics?

Chapter 3
School Dinners

"Wisdom is of more value than foolishness, just as light is better than darkness."

Ecclesiastes 2:13

"A society which is predominately Christian will propagate Christianity through its schools: one which is not, will not."

- C. S. Lewis

Why I Still Believe

An Entrée of Secularism

It is in some respects obvious and yet crucial for us not to forget that, though we all grow up in a *conditioning atmosphere,* this does not necessarily determine our approach to reality the rest of our lives. Indeed, it needs no proof that many who are brought up indifferent as skeptics or as atheists become Christians and many who are brought up in a Christian context become indifferent or skeptical. As C. S. Lewis asserts: "Religious education for children often has exactly the opposite effect to that which was intended; how many hardened atheists come from pious homes."[1]

As we grow and develop, many things influence us in a variety of ways. One of the most profound influences is our schooling. Here young minds are often changed as new ideas come to light.

Most people in my generation who grew up in England will have vivid memories of school dinners. In fact, we used to sing a playground jingle about them:

> Cooked school dinners, cooked school dinners
> Burnt baked beans, burnt baked beans
> Soggy semolina, soggy semolina
> I feel sick
> Get a bucket quick
> It's too late
> I've thrown up on my plate!

This somewhat vulgar rhyme summed up our collective view of these government-subsidized plates of fodder. I was put off "macaroni and cheese" for years due to these daily endurance tests. At twelve noon, we filed into the dining hall with our trays as though on a conveyor belt, holding out our plates at each "food station" for a heavy dollop of slop, usually served by a heavily built and "matron-like" dinner lady. We would

---

1   *Letters to an American Lady* (Grand Rapids: Eerdmans, 1967), 32.

not have looked out of place in prison-issue orange overalls.

I am evidently exaggerating the case, and should be grateful that we were eating a hot meal every day, but these early experiences have a way of lodging in the memory. There we were, like feeding time at the zoo, being physically fed and nourished. But it is not just food that we are fed during our school years. Our minds are nourished and nurtured also. We are often told that we are what we eat. Our diet determines a great deal about our physical health and shape. Likewise, our mental diet, what we are fed intellectually, begins to nurture and nourish a certain frame of mind, shaping our network of presuppositions and establishing our world view wittingly or unwittingly. As we develop, this cognitive diet has a profound impact upon our intellectual health and constitution.

On the whole I was like any other young student. I got into trouble at times – my worst offense was probably putting drawing pins under the soft seat cover of my history teacher's chair – yet I was also accused of being a "swot" (too concerned about learning). I loved sports and music. I went through a range of "career plans" from dreaming of professional soccer to zoology, the Royal Air Force, and criminal litigation. Growing up with three brothers there was rarely a dull moment and we charged through those early years and our teens with great zest for life. And I guess there were things about me that some would consider less "normal." I was a fairly serious and thoughtful young person, often reflecting on "ultimate issues." At times I would sit in the library and find myself contemplating Christianity and its concepts of eternity until my mind went blank, unable to comprehend. I would think about why I was me and not somebody else, what made me who I was. I would often try to imagine what the "invisible" God was like.

I loved books from a relatively early age and could spend hours in second-hand bookshops in the theology and philosophy sections. I recall one dusty old shop in my hometown called Darcies; I often got lost in there for an afternoon.

But the high school I attended was by no means Bible thumping. It was a large public (comprehensive in the UK) school that was a thoroughly indoctrinating place. I'm sure it thought of itself as "neutral" in religious matters and "tolerant," but from the age of twelve to eighteen, students' heads were filled with every evolutionary, naturalistic, and secular assumption that could be mustered. The metaphysical "certainty of uncertainty" was the basic underlying but unarticulated doctrine. The few nominally Christian teachers on the faculty were of the variety that did not really believe the Bible and so the mandatory "Christian element" in school life was a parody of the real, to say the least. While I studied here, there were perhaps a handful of students who would have called themselves Christians. Consequently, my experience at school was not easy. It represented vividly a constant clash of world views that were mutually incompatible. If ever the reality of "antithesis" between Christianity and non-Christian thought manifested itself to me, it was here.

Swimming upstream

At times I was the subject of ridicule and derision for my faith. I recall on one occasion some of my classmates, finding my school bag untended, wrote "666" all over it, and "we love the devil," and papered the classroom with similar vituperation. I was occasionally physically bullied for being a Christian – or at least being "different," as most of the antagonists would have had no understanding of the issues or why they were doing what they were doing. This was fairly easy to deal with. What was more difficult was the subtle but public derision I took from certain staff members. One particular geology teacher rarely missed an opportunity to hold my "creationist" convictions up to ridicule, misrepresenting the ideas and patronizing me to entertain the other students. Thus, it was here that my Christianity and "neutrality" came into sharp contrast.

It was a challenging as well as a formative time. When

faced with this sort of confrontation in life it is possible to go one of two ways. You can capitulate and go with the tide, abandoning your convictions without a fight, or you can re-examine your foundations (world view) to see if your convictions are justified and, if so, challenge the assumptions of those who are seeking to undermine or even ridicule that belief. I am thankful that I was able (by the grace of God) to choose that latter response; I know many who chose the former.

I also found these periods very emotionally draining and was at times despondent, being ostracized and apparently isolated from the thinking and behavioral patterns of so many others. I either had to "dig in" or compromise by being a shallow character, too cowardly to stand up for my faith and nail my colors to the mast! In some respects, my story might seem more "authentic" to you if I were able to say that at this point I went through terrible doubts about my faith, that as I became more "educated" I saw the inadequacy of Christianity, yet being stubborn as a mule, I somehow clung onto my faith as a shipwrecked man clutches at floating debris in the water. But to admit this would, for my part, be simply dishonest. Instead, I remained bemused by the empty character and practical inadequacy of the secular perspective lived out in the lives of many of my peers.

Gradually, I began to react strongly to this rampant humanism. Rather than being cowed by it, I found myself advancing against it! So true was this for me that one of my classmates in the sixth form (at the age of seventeen) referred to me one day as "a slap-in-the-face evangelist." Instead of being embarrassed or shy about my faith I felt the necessity of going on the offensive, as it were, maximizing the novelty value it apparently granted me by seeking to articulate my faith as well and often as I felt able. I did not accost fellow students in the corridors and attempt to cram Gideon Bibles down their throats. I simply mean that I was prepared to communicate my faith with others when asked or when appropriate opportunity was available. I did not shy away from openly challenging some of the bias and misunderstanding that came up in the class or common room conversations.

For many students, of course, there was little confrontation of this nature in school. The majority I knew found that the same "open-mindedness" or indifference that was fairly typical at home, the same "lack of bias," continued seamlessly throughout their education. There was rarely conflict or struggle, no real recognition of the nature of their imbibed belief system or the serious challenges to it – just the comfortable thought that they were learning to be modern, neutral, independent, "non-religious," and free!

It is statistically likely that you also went to a "neutral" school, where God was almost completely excluded from every realm of study except perhaps the odd class in world religions. But I hope it is now fairly obvious that to be neutral is impossible. The notion of pure objectivity or lack of bias is merely a specific type of bias. Jesus said, "he who is not for me is against me" (Matthew 12:30). To fail to acknowledge Christ as Lord of the universe and foundation of all truth is to have rejected Him as such.

He claims to be the Creator of the universe, the one who created you and me and sustains our very lives by His power. In such a case everything in this world has His branding iron burned onto it: He is the owner. To fail to honor Him as such and call it "neutrality" would then be patently absurd. If I have guests from England staying in my home, as we often do here in Canada, and they, seeing letters addressed to "the owner" in our kitchen, family pictures everywhere, and all our possessions, proceeding to eat our food and enjoy our hospitality, should sit down at our table and ask me, "Does this house belong to anyone?" and assert they would be "neutral" on such a question, I would think they had lost their mind. You see, if Christ is who He claims to be, and Scripture is God's Word, then the evidence for God must be plain and His reality everywhere evident to those capable of seeing it, to those willing to see it.

DECEPTIVE APPEARANCES

You may well ask me then why it does not appear *to you* that the God of the Bible is everywhere in evidence and refer me back to the philosopher Michael Scriven: "Atheism is obligatory in the absence of any evidence for God's existence." How am I to respond to such a statement? I could, of course, rehearse for you the *theistic proofs* I have read many times over the years and try to show you with various appeals to "facts" and "logic" that the "idea of a God" alone makes sense of the world in which we live. I could talk about the prime mover or the first cause as required for anything to exist. I could explain various arguments for design and from design, illustrating it from William Paley and his watch analogy, and then in modern times from the complexity of a single cell, showing that design is empirical and the impossibility of this system "evolving" a piece at a time. I could talk about our moral nature and recognition of a moral law and explain how this refers us back to God, how without Him objective morality would be impossible. In fact, I could expose you to the big guns of Christian apologetics and offer numerous metaphysical arguments, but I am not entirely convinced, however effective my penmanship, that you would be won over. I could work ever so hard at showing you how plausible Christian theism is. And in the process, I would really enjoy speaking about biblical history, archaeology, prophecy, and miracles that support the message and explain to you why Christ must have been raised from the dead from an historical perspective. These are all valuable and for some people helpful to a degree, and we could pile them high. But I have had limited success with these arguments over the years, if the "nature of facts" has not previously been dealt with.

Why? Because quite possibly, from your standpoint, from your philosophy of fact and proof I may already be speaking about what you have decided is not possible on the basis of your autonomous reasoning[2] and logic. As an apologist I can offer nothing that will alter that unless I ask you to consider the very building blocks of your thinking. In all probability, we do not agree about much at all; if we don't agree even about the nature of facts (i.e. created and controlled by God or not created and controlled by God), how can we agree about where those "facts" lead? One of us is in the Matrix, the other is not! I suspect you may have seen this very popular film or at least know if it. I think it provides a useful conceptual illustration at this point. For those in the Matrix (an illusory computer-generated reality for the mind), the character of reality is altogether different than it is for those who have been freed from it. Those in it are deluded and deceived, oblivious to their condition. In order to be free, they must be freed from the outside: someone must come into the Matrix and get them out. First, they must be convinced of the possibility that their unexamined assumptions about the reality they have accepted are false. Yet, until they have awoken in the real world, no amount of evidence can finally convince those trapped in the Matrix that their world is a complete illusion; they must literally "wake up" to reality. Cornelius Van Til reminds his readers of a poignant story:

> You have heard the story of the valley of the blind. A young man who was out hunting fell over a precipice into the valley of the blind. There was no escape. The blind men did not understand him when he spoke of seeing the sun and the colors of the rainbow, but a fine young lady did understand him when he spoke the language of love. The father of the girl would not consent to the marriage of his daughter to a lunatic who spoke so often of things that did not exist. But

---

2   Autonomous reasoning is the kind that assumes its own self-sufficiency and independence apart from God. It assumes itself to be the ultimate criterion and authority for what is or is not true or possible while taking for granted that abstract reasoning allows us to "know things." It fails to ask what use of reason itself presupposes.

the great psychologists of the blind men's university offered to cure him of his lunacy by sewing up his eyelids. Then, they assured him, he would be normal like "everybody" else. But the simple seer went on protesting that he did see the sun.[3]

I also must protest for, to me, the evidence for God is plain and abundant. What then is the Christian explanation for why many people do not believe and follow Christ? Why is it that people so often refuse the evidences in creation and of the Bible? Why do we ignore or reject the account of reality given in Scripture? Jesus tells us it is because we are blinded by sin. And the truth that we *do know* internally about God as the Creator and ourselves as creatures, responsible to Him, we *suppress* in our desire for sovereignty (authority and rule) over our own lives – we hold down the truth in ethical hostility to God. Thus we opt for our so-called "neutrality" and "open-mindedness." A position, as we have seen, that is an illusion, built upon an implicit or explicit rejection of God's revelation. The apostle Paul writes in Romans 1:18-23:

> But God shows his anger from heaven against all sinful, wicked people who push the truth away from themselves. For the truth about God is known to them instinctively. God has put this knowledge in their hearts. From the time the world was created, people have seen the earth and sky and all that God made. They can clearly see his invisible qualities – his eternal power and divine nature. So they have no excuse whatsoever for not knowing God. Yes, they knew God, but they wouldn't worship him as god or even give him thanks. And they began to think up foolish ideas of what God was like. The result was that their minds became dark and confused. Claiming to be wise, they became utter fools instead. And instead of worshipping the glorious, ever-living God, they wor-

---

3   Cornelius Van Til, "Why I believe in God."

shiped idols made to look like mere people, or birds and animals and snakes.

I suggest to you that no one is neutral toward God or Scripture: we are already committed. Christianity shamelessly teaches that people without Christ are blind and they need their eyes opened to their true condition.

A Shocking Diagnosis

For some of us, this sort of strong and unequivocal statement of the apostle Paul is difficult to entertain. It might even be perceived as insulting. But consider this: a friend of mine recently started to get regular and severe nose bleeds for no apparent reason. Eventually he decided he ought to go to the doctor. The prognosis was shocking for a man in his early thirties. He was told he had dangerously high blood pressure and was at real and imminent risk of a heart attack if he did not radically change his lifestyle. He was informed in no uncertain terms that he was clinically obese, had a poor diet, and took insufficient exercise. The doctor warned him that, should he fail to pay attention to his instructions, the serious ramifications would be no one's fault but his own. My friend had been living oblivious to his condition and so blinded to its cause. Was the doctor trying to insult or offend him when he revealed the ailment, exposed the cause of his condition, and forced him to recognize it? Not at all! The doctor's Hippocratic Oath to put the health and wellbeing of the patient before any other consideration was his motivating principle.

In the same way, Christ's motivation in speaking and revealing the truth is not to insult us; He does so to preserve our very lives, for our good and wellbeing. My own motivation in writing this book is not to offend but to enlighten and seek ultimately the salvation and blessing of the reader. I am not offering you my musings and reflections as though I have some independent wisdom and authority to tell you how things really are. I am merely seeking to explain to you what Christ reveals in Scripture and how he has impacted my life. So, in the final analysis any dispute you have with the biblical diagnosis of the human condition is not with me but with Christ – He is the source of authority. Don't shoot the postman if the content of the letter is shocking!

I understand that in our relativistic and apparently "tolerant" society it is disconcerting to be confronted with a message that is so forthright, uncompromising, and exclusive – as all *truth claims* must be by definition. Part of the problem with today's notion of "tolerance" is its incoherence, requiring the *equal validity (truthfulness)* of all views. Thus, when it comes to the truth claims of Christianity (or any other truth claim) it requires you to be open-minded and closed-minded both at the same time, a psychological impossibility! The twenty-first century secular individual must profess this open-mindedness, whilst being utterly closed to the absolute truth claims of Christ.

It is certainly true that Christ's life and message were deeply offensive to many in the first century: as you read on you will find out why. For the sake of argument put yourself in my shoes, upon the Christian world view. Follow the argument through even if the biblical message makes you uncomfortable. Sometimes it is beneficial to be irritated for our own sake; it stirs us and forces us to think about our assumptions and behavior. This exercise is never wasted time. Indeed, Scripture tells us that if we earnestly examine these matters and seek the truth with integrity we will see for ourselves how "wisdom is of more value than foolishness, just as light is better than darkness."

Define and explain these words and phrases:

1. Antithesis
2. Autonomy
3. Neutrality

Answer the following questions:

1. Explain Van Til's "Valley of the Blind" illustration. (p. 70-71)
2. How does your early life and childhood compare to Joe's?
3. How do your core beliefs now compare to the beliefs in the environment where you were raised? Can you identify a time when you made a conscious decision to reject or affirm any of the beliefs you were raised with?
4. According to Joe, what is involved in 'being a Christian'? How does this compare to other descriptions you may have heard or assumed?

Chapter 4

Ridicule and Rebuttals!

*"Only fools say in their hearts,
'There is no God.'
They are corrupt . . .
The* Lord *looks down from heaven
on the entire human race;
he looks to see if there is even one with real understanding,
one who seeks for God."*

Psalm 14:1-2

"Brief and powerless is man's life; on him and all his race the slow, sure doom falls pitiless and dark. Blind to good and evil, reckless of destruction, omnipotent matter rolls on its relentless way."

- Bertrand Russell

Why I Still Believe

Later schooling – skepticism for dessert

It may seem at this point that I must have been lacking in some area of "rudimentary" education. After all, how is it possible in the twenty-first century to believe in the antiquated notion of the God of the Bible? Surely anyone who has been exposed in any degree to modern science or a smattering of contemporary philosophy must reject such an archaic view? Perhaps a god of some sort exists; after all, this is an "open" universe insofar as anything is possible, but the God of the Bible? Surely not! Such a God is so offensive to our post-modern sensibilities. He is so politically incorrect. In truth, I could be writing about almost any other conception of God and most people would not be offended in the slightest.

But the God of the Christian Scriptures is utterly unacceptable. He is a God who called creation into existence from nothing, rather than being part of the universe Himself, in the trees, the rivers, and us. He is the God who is self-contained and needs nothing from human beings, who created them in *His* image to know Him and His mind, to worship and enjoy Him forever, rather than being a god we can mold to our image and preferences. He is the God who will not compromise, giving binding moral commandments and holding human beings to account, rather than an impersonal god, an abstract principle without moral awareness, or a vague benevolent spirit who just wants everybody to have a good time doing as they please. He is the God who is sovereign, guiding all things in His providence according to the counsel of His will, by infinite wisdom. He is the one who governs all things according to His exhaustive eternal plan, rather than a finite god, struggling to interpret this universe – like all those who reason without an absolute God. He is not caught in a "continuum" of matter and energy with humanity, caught in the chaos, a "god" the same as us. He is the God who alone claims to speak with absolute authority and limits human beings to "finding" reality as He has made it rather than "legislating" what reality can and cannot be as competing "lords" over and against any god.

For many, this conception of the God revealed in the Bible just will not do. Such a God is too offensive to independent reason, too restrictive, too hostile toward a variety of lifestyle choices. I have picked the worst sort of God to put faith in, in these "tolerant" times. I have failed to be sensitive to the reader by showing a breadth of appreciation for other conceptions of God. You may be wondering what sort of religious fanatic or draconian creature still believes in the God of the "pre-moderns."

Have I never heard of Charles Darwin and macro evolution? Do I not realize that the Bible has been disproved – Richard Dawkins says so! Have I been living on Mars for the last thirty years? Have I not encountered the work of David Hume, Immanuel Kant, Friedrich Nietzsche, Karl Marx, Aldous Huxley, Antony Flew, or Bertrand Russell? Am I unaware of French existentialism? What of Camus, Sartre, and Derrida? Do I not realize that such people, and many other thinkers, have shown the inadequacy of arguments for God, the miraculous and biblical history? Have I not heard that "God is dead," that religion is just the opium of the people? Have I not understood that all religious language is meaningless or that Christianity is not empirically verifiable? Surely I am conscious of the loneliness of humankind in the universe, that all is meaningless, and life is only what I define it to be or make of it? Humankind has the power of choice now, a freedom without purpose, to no end. We alone determine what is right and wrong, true and false. Humankind has come of age, we are autonomous, free, self-determining. And surely I understand that history itself and all religious claims are mere *power plays* to control and manipulate others. All is *relative*; there can be no objectivity in history: that's objectively certain! There are no absolutes, and that's absolutely final! It's all a matter of personal interpretation, what's true for you isn't necessarily true for me. Joe Boot, you really have been living in a box, you are so behind the times! Your parents merely passed on to you their human projection of a "father figure" due to their insecurity and poor relationship with their parents; what you now depend on as a "god" is a psychological disorder, Freud taught us that. No I'm afraid this biblical conception of God will not be tolerated in our tolerant society, it's back to school for you, Joe Boot.

Most people, in reality, know very little about the Bible and, consequently, little about the sovereign God I have been describing. The prejudicial conjecture that swirls around our popular culture about Christianity, in a climate of biblical illiteracy, leads to much misunderstanding and confusion. However, the suspicion of "non-exposure" to secular thought and counter arguments to Christianity in my case would be completely incorrect. In fact I was, and have since been, exposed, more than most, to pretty much every major objection to Christian theism that has been raised. Indeed, as a vocational Christian apologist I have been dealing with such objections and questions in lectures, debates, and question-and-answer sessions for many years from people as diverse as taxi drivers to professors of philosophy at world-class universities. I have close work colleagues on five continents who regularly come together to compare notes on questions and objections raised to Christianity. I spend numerous hours every year speaking at universities, colleges, conferences, and at various business or professional events to skeptics and inquirers about these matters. Unfortunately, time and space do not allow me to offer a detailed rebuttal to the characters and specific issues raised above, but I will be summarizing what they all share in common shortly and will offer the Christian response in the appropriate place.

My preparation for the life of an apologist described above began in my school days when I read philosophy and history of Christianity. Of course, at this point I had little idea that I was being "prepared" for anything, but I have come to believe in a God who is completely sovereign, who orchestrated my environment as a young man, who also planned the conversion of my parents and who has guided and molded you to the point where you are reading this book. God has a purpose in it – that is what I believe.

My philosophy teacher was a confirmed atheist and he made no secret of the fact that his intention was to turn our small group of six students into logical positivists – that is a school of thought, stemming in modern times from a group of philosophers in Vienna, which held that all statements about God (in fact, metaphysics of any kind) were meaningless as they cannot be empirically[1] verified. Only those statements that *could* be empirically verified have a meaning. The trouble is that the "verification principle" itself cannot be empirically verified. Whoever *observed* that only empirically justified statements have a meaning?

This view, which is still popular, is evidently self-defeating and self-contradictory. When we do science (empirical investigation) we are describing an "event" of sense perception. However, as soon as we move beyond *description* of a particular instance to affirm what is going to happen in the future, our work has become *prescriptive* – something science does all of the time to be of any practical use. But these *prescriptions* of, say, natural law (which are really descriptive) are no longer empirical observations: they are metaphysical assumptions about patterns, order, and uniformity, which cannot be proved empirically.

It was the British philosopher David Hume, himself an empiricist, who really highlighted this. To take particular instances of a thing or event and then extrapolate to reach a general (wider) conclusion is called the "inductive method." But Hume showed that empirically (in a universe without God) we have no right to expect "science" to work – we are, after all, just a "bundle of sensations." He ended up denying

---

1   Empirical investigation is the bedrock of the scientific method that gives primacy to sense experience in the acquisition of knowledge – the logical positivists sought to rule out all other forms of knowledge as meaningful or significant.

we could really know anything about reality at all! When the logical positivist reasons and applies logic in trying to support his empiricism he is employing principles that are not empirically derived! These principles, like the laws of logic and math, must simply be assumed or presupposed, to allow reasoning to work at all. Some have sought to get around the empirical problem by saying it must be that matter has "emergent properties" that produce logic and uniformity, but this is plain old question-begging. The question is, how do you know? We can't say with any certainty what the properties of matter actually are! The real question is, *why* does the universe appear to allow the inductive method to work? *Why* can we apply logic, mathematical laws and reason to this world and have success? To employ logic, reason, and empirical observation to support a defense of empiricism that claims "matter just has these properties" is merely to presuppose the validity of the empirical process and the validity of my reasoning, not to justify or account for it. Nonetheless, this was the atmosphere of my later schooling where we dealt in detail with the philosophy of religion.

My teacher knew my persuasions and so regularly targeted Christianity with scurrilous outbursts. During this two-year period I was exposed not only to the traditional arguments for Christianity but the arguments against Christianity mustered by modern philosophy in metaphysics, epistemology, and ethics. I heard them from a teacher who professed to believe that, in light of some of these objections, Christianity proved untenable. Later I heard them expounded by professors and apologists who believed, on the contrary, that non-Christian philosophies were incoherent and self-refuting showing that philosophical attacks against Christian theism cannot be plausibly sustained; some of them had formulated powerful responses to such objections themselves.

It was during these studies that I started a Christian Student Union in the school that began with three of us, including one of my brothers. Each Tuesday after school I would go to the staff room and put a notice in every teacher's file to read at roll call announcing the time and subject for the following day's Christian meeting during lunch hour. My first proper series of talks was called "Science and the Bible," in which I sought, with limited skill, to counter naturalistic evolutionary arguments. During my school days I, like all other students, went through the standard evolutionary indoctrination process, involving outdated and even fabricated evidence that had already been exposed as fraudulent. For example, teachers still used Ernst Haeckel's drawings of embryos, faked to infer that all living creatures, including human beings, possessed fish-like "gill slits" as a throwback to common evolutionary ancestry. Or the peppered moth fraud, where moths were *pinned* to trees in an attempt to prove evolution – an argument which, even had it been legitimate research, showed nothing more than *variation* within the species. Though I was inexperienced and had done limited reading at this stage, the Christian Union became a success. By the time I left the school there were over twenty students regularly meeting at lunch time despite the overall atmosphere of the school, from the headmaster down, being distinctly anti-Christian.

During this period, I had opportunity to consider the main arguments against Christianity from atheists and skeptics, but upon discussion, reflection, reading, and prayer I personally found them inadequate. Indeed, I found more than satisfying reasons to trust the authority and truthfulness of the Bible. I discovered nothing at that time in either the assumptions of naturalistic science or secular philosophy that appeared to threaten the "fortress of Christian theism." In fact, I found that my faith and confidence in the Christ of Scripture grew during this period.

To illustrate, before I studied the philosophy of religion I was largely unaware of the many brilliant men and women that littered the history of the church. I had never before encountered the sterling defense of the Christian faith offered by people like Augustine of Hippo, St. Anselm, Thomas Aquinas, Blaise Pascal, Joseph Butler, William Paley, John Locke, Jonathan Edwards, Søren Kierkegaard and many others. It was a real eye-opener and encouragement for me to see how many people of great genius not only believed in Christ but vigorously and passionately defended that belief. I saw very clearly that the popular conception of Christians as people who must throw away their brain as they enter a church building to worship was a heinous fabrication. This exposure to so many great Christian minds from the past was a richly rewarding and strengthening experience. I found many things among these thinkers powerful and compelling. So, to a large extent, the opposite result came from my philosophy teacher's intentions. I was built up and strengthened in my faith and in my own personal spiritual life. The Bible came alive to me in new ways speaking directly to the issues raised in philosophy (offering a specifically Christian philosophy), and my relationship with God deepened through the whole experience.

It was during my second year of these studies that I decided to go on to theological college. By this time I was sensing a strong desire to serve God in Christian evangelism. I would say that I felt "called," even compelled, by God. The all-conditioning one had been preparing and shaping me, so at eighteen I headed for a theological college in Birmingham, England.

Ridicule and Rebuttals!

Define and explain these words and phrases:

1. Empiricism
2. Descriptive
3. Prescriptive

Answer the following questions:

1. What are the strongest or most plausible objections you've heard against Christianity? How have you responded?
2. What are the major objections that Joe outlines in this chapter? Are they similar to or different from the objections you might hear from your peers today?
3. Have you experienced ridicule of your beliefs? How would you respond to the claim that your beliefs are out of step with 'neutral' or 'objective' reality?
4. Many of the prominent intellectuals in Western philosophy are not orthodox Christians. Why do you think that is? Does that make you reconsider the Christian perspective? Do you believe Christianity has intellectual credibility, or is it a matter of 'faith'?

Chapter 5
Boot Camp

"To increase knowledge only increases sorrow."
Ecclesiastes 1:18

"[Education is] that which discloses to the wise and disguises from the foolish their lack of understanding."
- Ambrose Bierce

Sojourns at Seminary

I spent the next three years in further theological and philosophical study. For the first two of these, I was at an old-fashioned and traditional theological college, established not merely for academic study but to train and prepare young men and women for pastoral, evangelistic, and missionary work. I will never forget the day I arrived, finding my creaking, weathered room at the top of a 200-year-old house with pigeons living in the roof. I can best describe this institute as "Boot Camp" for "Onward Christian soldiers!" It was much more than an academic college. Here I received my basic training in handling the tools of our trade and the weapons of spiritual war.

The first thing I discovered was how ignorant I really was in so many ways. In part, this was just my youth, but it was also due to the fact that a quality education should always make us aware (if we are wise) of how little we really do know of our subject and of life as a whole. At a military boot camp new soldiers become quickly aware that their "fitness level" will need bringing up and that they are unprepared, at first, for the gruesome task of war. But steadily fitness increases. They learn to handle rifles, shooting accurately at the target as well as becoming familiar with other military equipment and basic battle strategy. Whilst the analogy is imperfect, it goes some way to describe what seminary was like for me. I began to learn how to use the tools of a Christian epistemology and to handle Scripture correctly (hermeneutics). I also got a firm handle on the metaphysical structure (ultimate scheme and conceptual framework) of the Christian world view.

The "daily drill" was not far off a military ideal. The average day began early at 6:30 am for house prayers followed by time for personal prayer. Then it was breakfast and chores before chapel prayers with the entire student body at 9 am. The rest of the morning was spent in lectures with free time, chores, or practical ministry in the afternoons depending on the day of the week. After dinner, from 6 to 9 pm, was compulsory study – though I regularly flouted this particular rule for weight training at a friend's gym! Some would consider this quite a regimen. Today's university student might suspect I was out of my mind for choosing such a "limiting" environment at the age of eighteen. Nonetheless, I enjoyed those years immensely and would not have changed them for the world as I rose to the lofty heights (or top of the slippery pole according to the principal!) of head student within eighteen months – a dubious privilege, but a democratic process!

Here I was being taught by Christian professors and this time I heard theological and philosophical arguments, but from a different perspective. It was here also that I heard the liberal (as well as the orthodox) view of Scripture laid out. I considered the arguments and read many involved discussions. I read scholars who sat in judgment upon Scripture, assessing its credibility based upon their own unargued philosophical bias of what was possible and what was not. They maintained that if Christianity was to survive in the fast-developing modern world it would have to abandon a super-naturalist world view and all claims to the miraculous; people, they told us, could not buy this anymore! Christianity would have to compromise with secular philosophy and adapt itself to comment only upon spiritual, emotional, and personal matters of "faith" (to the secularist a world akin to make-believe). It must confine itself to speculating about the *why* and never speak about the *what* or *how* of reality! It must, in effect, sign a truce, a peace treaty, a ceasefire, a pact with the devil, agreeing that humanism (secularism) and its "science" should be granted *neutrality* in the realm of knowledge and henceforth must not be challenged. This so-called "science" and "religion" must be separated – they are "non-overlapping magisteria." Christianity could still have a voice in the world so long as it avoided talking about facts, history, and science. Let Christianity deal with the realm of spirituality, for those inclined that way, and let the men and women of science deal with the "facts." Of course, if you allow this separation, you have already conceded that the Christian world view is false.

I also read about their *hypothetical* "sources" for the Old Testament. The theory was dubbed the "documentary hypothesis" (the idea that many writers separated by generations provided the source documents for Scripture), yet in academic circles it quickly became almost heretical to *question* this "hypothesis." Although these so-called "sources" have never been found, scholars often wrote about such hypothetical documents as though they actually existed. *Prejudicial conjecture* seemed to be the basic logical fallacy that undermined their assertions. They happily assumed that the Bible was not the work of the authors Scripture claimed, and they came up with their arbitrary reasons for endless rationalizations. The writings of these apologists for liberalism would often attack or even deride evangelicals and reformed thinkers, exhorting them to "change or die out." But again I found their ideas far from compelling. I listened to my very able professors offering solid rebuttals of their arguments, certainly sufficient to satisfy me that these "higher critics" were not neutral scholars, but profoundly misguided, and that I could trust the Scriptures as the Word of God.

Within fifteen years that same liberalism I was exposed to, that believed it was rescuing the Church from becoming obsolete, is already passé. Today it is increasingly consigned to the reject bin of scholastic fads. Perhaps more noticeably, those denominations and churches that bought into this old liberalism "hook, line, and sinker" are the ones at death's door. Around the world today it is the Bible-believing churches that are growing by leaps and bounds as the old liberals close down week by week in their last gasp. Of course, a new form of liberalism is slowly coming to the surface; this is to be expected, but it too will rise and fall. So, in my life as a theological student, I again heard a fairly full statement of various secular and humanistic forms of unbelief (with or without a religious garb) and their best attacks upon the biblical edifice.

Boot Camp

Define and explain these words and phrases:

1. Liberalism
2. Humanism
3. Prejudicial conjecture

Answer the following questions:

1. Explain the term 'non-overlapping magisteria.' What are some of the implications of this belief in the relationship of 'science' and 'religion?' Can you think of a different way to express this viewpoint? How would you respond if someone posed this argument?
2. In this chapter Joe talks about the liberalism that he was exposed to while at school. Are we seeing the same type of liberalism today? (p. 89-90)
3. Joe explains the logical fallacy of prejudicial conjecture. What are some other common logical fallacies that come up in arguments both for and against orthodox Christianity?

Chapter 6
No Apology

"Always be ready to give a defense to everyone who asks you a reason for the hope that is in you, with meekness and fear."

1 Peter 3:15 NKJV

"Faith is not blind faith . . . Christianity can be shown to be, not 'just as good as' or even 'better than' the non-Christian position, but the only position that does not make nonsense of human experience."

- Cornelius Van Til

Offering an apology

When the ancient Greek philosopher Socrates was accused of atheism and corrupting the youth of Athens, Plato tells us that in a courtroom speech, Socrates offered an "apology." This did not mean that he accepted the charges and said "sorry" to all present for his inappropriate beliefs or behavior; on the contrary, it meant that he offered a *defense* (*apologia*) of the integrity and justness of his position! Unfortunately, Socrates was eventually sentenced to death.

I have spent many years now as a Christian evangelist and apologist seeking to defend, justify, and explain the Christian philosophy of life. I have done my best to show that all truth is located in Christ and His Word and that this truth is objective, absolute, and certain. This may sound incredibly arrogant to you and I suppose it would be if Christ was not who He claimed to be. However, I believe He *must* be who He claims and therefore I am compelled to make the message of the Bible known as the authoritative revelation of God through my apologetic – but with no apology! I am not "sorry" about the truth. And I am not sorry that I am required to speak the truth. However, I am often sorry about the way I have, at times, failed to represent Christ properly both by my attitude in, and method of, defending His cause. And I am sorry about the way that at times in the contemporary and historic Church many claiming the title "Christian" have grossly misrepresented Him and distorted the biblical message. So it is incumbent upon me on certain occasions to express my sorrow at these failures, but I can never apologize for the sinless Christ, His claims or message.

In the line of fire

During my vocation I have experienced numerous barrages from the secular philosophical guns. I have endured skepticism's heavy artillery bombarding me on a regular basis. As suggested when writing about my "boot camp" years of preparation, it can feel like a life of intellectual and spiritual combat. And indeed it is, in the clash of world views, the world of ideas both concrete and abstract. I am often found in front of many people – especially university students, in open forums or on radio and television debates – or simply talking with my neighbors.

One of the "shells" most often fired to dislodge the Christian platform in such settings is the dogma re-introduced more radically in modern times by the German philosopher Immanuel Kant and developed further by the logical positivists I discussed earlier. Kant divided reality into two realms, the phenomenal (that which can be experienced through the five senses) and the noumenal (beyond the senses). Conscious of the problems (transcendental failure) of both rationalism and empiricism, he attempted a synthesis of the two in order to rescue reason, science, and meaning – including morality. Kant's astonishing basic contention was that we can only know things about the realm of phenomena (what can be discovered by the senses), and since this phenomenal realm is processed by our minds which *impose* forms of intuition upon reality (i.e. causality, substance, space, and time) we cannot know reality as it really is in itself – we can only know how it appears to us. Consequently, knowledge is really only an incomplete knowledge of oneself, so people become the very creators of reality, a reality existing in the mind. But because reason has limits, he left room for a god that could not be known or reveal himself. As a result, Kant turns science into a form of psychology and faith into a type of mysticism.

So confident was Kant in his rational autonomy that he felt able to slice up reality, legislating for others what can and cannot be known on his own authority! God could not have spoken in Christ Jesus or in the revelation of Scripture: for Kant no theoretical knowledge of God is even possible. But to say we *cannot know* God, that reality itself *cannot be known*, is to say a great deal about God and a great deal about reality.

It is in fact to claim an exhaustive knowledge. Kant's artificial distinctions (reality as it is in itself versus reality as we perceive or shape it) are arbitrary as he attempts to rescue empiricism and rationalism. How can Kant possibly know what reality is or is not in itself? How can he possibly know what can or cannot be known of God? Only by a clear insight into his so-called noumenal realm, of which, he tells us, nothing can be known! In Kant's thought, proud rationalism reached a zenith, and yet is destroyed on its own terms! How could Kant *know* that reality as his mind interpreted it bears any relation to anybody else's mind? His philosophy becomes a purely subjective form of psychology, destroying the possibility of objective meaning in anything – including his own work.

If you recall, the positivists (picking up some of Kant's affirmations), among other schools, insisted that you simply cannot have a real knowledge of anything that is beyond empirical investigation. If it cannot be verified by the senses it cannot be verified at all – this leads to what we may call "hostility to metaphysics." This hostility is rooted in the idea that you cannot reason from the world of sense to the world beyond the senses: to do so is to talk gibberish – you simply cannot know what you cannot "test" by means of sense perceptions. This view is not confined to academic or philosophical circles; it has filtered down to become a state of mind for many educated people in various vocations and professions. It is all too easily assumed that to speak of God, creation, miracles, providence and a transcendent moral law is akin to speaking of fairies, Santa Claus and the Easter Bunny. We simply cannot know anything outside the "phenomenal world;" any belief one has about existences "beyond physics" is subjective and relative to the individual, a matter of preference and without foundation.

But when we examined the assumptions behind this hostility we saw, ironically, that it is *impossible to avoid* metaphysical commitments. To say that *"nothing can be known that transcends our temporal experience"* is to make a universal statement about reality, concerning the limits of possibility and the "great scheme of things" – all such statements are metaphysical statements (faith statements) in nature! It then boils down to a choice: what is our metaphysic going to be? But how do we decide? Friedrich Nietzsche, with refreshing intellectual honesty, observes with respect to philosophers:

> They all pose as if they had discovered and reached their real opinions through self-development of a cold, pure, divinely unconcerned dialectic...while at bottom it is an assumption, a hunch, indeed a kind of inspiration – most often a desire of the heart that has been filtered and made abstract – that they defend with reasons they have sought after the fact. They are all advocates who resent that name, and for the most part even wily spokesmen for their prejudices which they baptize 'truth'.... Gradually it has become clear to me what every great philosophy so far has been: namely, the personal confession of its author and a kind of involuntary and unconscious memoir; also that the moral (or immoral) intentions of every philosophy constituted the real germ of life from which the whole plant had grown.[1]

In other words, he suggests the works of the philosophers (which must include his own work to be consistent) are memoirs and confessions of their own moral preferences, based on assumptions arbitrarily chosen, out of a heart manifesting a bedlam of desires! So, he suggests, our metaphysical commitments are almost always ethically driven!

The Bible affirms the ethical root of our presuppositions when it tells us that our minds, since the Fall of our first parents, have indulged in hostility toward God and His moral requirements. We are hopelessly biased in our metaphysical

---

1   Friedrich Nietzsche, "On the Prejudice of Philosophers," in *Beyond Good and Evil*, trans. Walter Kaufmann (New York: Vintage Books, 1966), 12, 13.

choices seeking to *suppress (hold down)* rather than uncover the truth.

When this barrage of ethical hostility is fired in the form of empiricism (logical positivism, scientism and skepticism) I find it essential to challenge the interlocutor to look at this unargued philosophical bias. For a start, many scientifically minded people who readily adopt this view of reality forget the fact that scientists themselves reason from the seen to the unseen all the time in seeking workable models in science. Cast your mind back to my illustration concerning the big bang hypothesis. This theory is laden with "hypothetical entities" to provide a model that has not been empirically verified, and yet it is considered practically "law" by many in the scientific community and amongst the general public. This sort of double standard should not be acceptable when considering competing truth claims.

Furthermore, I should reiterate that the Christian faith is not "bottom up" but "top down" in its understanding of reality. The God of the Bible reveals Himself in Scripture (verbal revelation) and in His creation, to communicate with His creatures so that they are not left with their arbitrary speculations. People do not *demonstrate* God by *reasoning up* from their empirical observations – God reveals Himself. Then, as we accept on faith (presuppose) the authority of God's revelation we see that it alone can account for reason, science, logic, language and morality, in fact any meaningful experience at all. It is then recognizable as the very pre-condition of intelligibility, the only foundation that makes sense of human experience or justifies our most basic beliefs necessary for us to function in this world.

If the God of the Bible exists, then how can God's self-disclosure be seen as impossible, in the created realm or in His Word? The empiricist has just assumed that all knowledge can only come via the senses – precluding, for example, a real knowledge of history or the universe – and consequently they *must* reject Christianity. They do not demonstrate their assumption that *"all significant knowledge is empirical in nature;"* where is the evidence for this? This statement itself cannot be empirically verified as it asserts a *universal* and *necessary* dogma that must *control* investigation, not a contingent historical observation that leads to a temporal conclusion.

Thus, we see again that it falls by its own standard. There is no way to verify empirically that all knowledge is empirical in nature for the simple reason that, *if* all knowledge is *not* empirically derived (the point in question), such knowledge (arrived at by means other than a purely empirical process), being "above" the senses, could be neither affirmed nor denied empirically. So, this sort of pompous empiricism and scientism, being the natural offspring of Kant and the positivists, shows itself to be an arbitrary position, resting on unargued philosophical bias that leads inexorably to skepticism.

A SCIENTIFIC DESTRUCTION OF SCIENCE

All of us tempted to swallow this popular pill, cunningly served up with our secular education, should appreciate that the empiricists have not shown that the Creator has not spoken in His creation or in the Christ of Scripture. In the process of their argument they annihilate empirical science itself, the very thing that they have put their faith in. Science depends upon the "non-empirical" ideas of uniformity in nature and the predictability of future events in order to function or teach us anything. But empirical verification must apply only to a particular time, place and entity to be examined. I cannot empirically prove that the sun will rise tomorrow until I test the hypothesis tomorrow! The past cannot be used as a basis for predicting the future if no metaphysical truths are valid – science as we know it would then become impossible! Knowledge (science) could mean no more than the reception of unrelated and therefore unintelligible sensations, bombarding the senses from the physical world.

Remember also that my opponent, in arguing against

me for empiricism, is utilizing tools of logic and reasoning through which he or she is suggesting that my argument for Christianity is invalid. But these rules, criteria and propositions are not empirical in nature either – they are metaphysical (abstract, immaterial and universal). Since when has anyone seen, smelt or touched the logical law of the excluded middle?[2] Thus, reasoning itself is destroyed as the human mind is reduced to a random collection of atoms and electro-chemical events which we cannot assume is anything more than a "statistical anomaly." We cannot even speak of the brain revealing a "pattern" if all knowledge is purely empirical. And then who is to say that the atomic *event* constituting my brain leading me to believe in Jesus Christ is any more or less "valid" than the atomic *event* of your brain leading you to put faith in empiricism? The "validity" of any argument involves an appeal to various metaphysical (transcendent) criteria. For example, how do we know that to be an empiricist is valid? That is a metaphysical question. A material event accessible to the senses is neither valid nor invalid, it is just an event.

In my experience the person who takes this view has rarely seen that they too are metaphysicians, they too are people of faith. They presuppose their materialism, universally limiting the nature of existence, without any warrant (empirical or otherwise) to do so! Consequently, by metaphysics we seek to disprove metaphysics. In the end the person holding this view has undermined the very possibility of any knowledge at all, whereas Christianity provides us with the basis for knowledge, logic and the intelligibility of our experience.

In these exchanges, conversations and discussions I have found that the foundation of Scripture and Christian truth have never failed me yet. I say this to reiterate again that I have heard what has been said against the Christian faith by

---

2   A foundational law of logic identifying that if something is true, this excluded something (falsity). If "X is true" then "not-X" is false. For example: I either am a man, or I am not a man – no third way is possible. Or to illustrate again, God either exists or He does not exist – there is no middle option.

non-Christian skeptics many times, and I have only become further convinced of the truth concerning Christ and His Word. My colleagues who work across the world at this task find our testimony is the same.

It has been in the days since my formal education that I have delved deeper and deeper into various apologetical issues. I have made a detailed study of evolutionary thought and published at the popular level on the subject of the philosophy of science and the critical problems with evolutionary theory. These things cannot be discussed in detail here, but there are numerous brilliant scholarly works on the reliability of Scripture, the canon and the ancient documents as well as on science and creation, miracles, biblical prophecy, the human predicament, Christian epistemology and the resurrection of Christ, to mention but a few.

I am certainly not saying that I have personally solved all the difficulties with respect to Christian theism and the revelation of God in Scripture. In fact, my belief in Jesus Christ demands that there is mystery involved in the human experience for the good reason that all things find their ultimate explanation in God who is self-contained. This means He is infinite (without limits, beginning or end), incontingent (dependent upon nothing and no one for His being, character or nature), omniscient (all-knowing because all-controlling), omnipotent (all-powerful), tri-personal (an eternal community consisting of one God in three persons) and consequently incomprehensible. He is only *apprehensible* because He has revealed Himself to us in Christ and in His Word. So, there is no one you or I will ever find who can explain all things to us, for whom reality is transparent, because God alone has that epistemic advantage – He is the infinite, only wise God. As the Scriptures say:

> Oh, what a wonderful God we have! How great are his riches and wisdom and knowledge! How impossible it is for us to understand his decisions and his methods! For who can know what the Lord is thinking? Who

knows enough to be his counselor? And who could ever give him so much that he would have to pay it back? For everything comes from him; everything exists by his power and is intended for his glory. To him be glory evermore. Amen. (Romans 11:33-36)

Because this God lives, it is my conviction that only those who recognize the lordship (kingship) of Christ in their thinking can find any explanation for anything at all. It is this bold claim that I will now seek to support.

No Apology

Define and explain these words and phrases:

1. Metaphysics
2. Phenomenal
3. Noumenal

Answer the following questions:

1. Summarize Kant's main argument (p. 95-96)
2. Why is it impossible to avoid metaphysical commitments? (p. 96)
3. What presuppositions do metaphysicians hold? Outline some other basic presuppositions that various philosophies might hold. (p. 99-100)
4. What does Joe mean when he says that "the Christian faith is not "bottom up" but "top down" in its understanding of reality"? What are the implications of this distinction?

Chapter 7
The Heart of the Matter

"Christ is the visible image of the invisible God. He existed before God made anything at all and is supreme over all creation. Christ is the one through whom God created everything in heaven and earth. He made the things we can see and the things we can't see – kings, kingdoms, rulers, and authorities. Everything has been created through him and for him. He existed before everything else began, and he holds all creation together."

Colossians 1:15-17

"[C]onsider not only the consequences which flow from a given hypothesis, but the consequences which flow from denying the hypothesis . . . you must look at what follows from the thing supposed, and to any other things which you choose . . ."

-Plato

Why I Still Believe

The Problem of Philosophy

I want now to try and summarize the position of the non-Christian and outline something of the Christian response to it. It is essential that we consider the consequences which flow from a denial or affirmation of Christian and non-Christian thought. None of us should be daunted by "philosophy." It was the French atheist Voltaire who humorously quipped concerning his occupation: "When he who listens does not know what he who speaks means, and when he who speaks does not know what he himself means, that's philosophy." I will try to avoid these typical pitfalls as we take a brief look at the foundational issues.

The word "philosophy" is related to two Greek words: philo meaning "love" and sophia meaning "wisdom." It simply means to "love wisdom." Every human being is a philosopher to some degree and necessarily has a philosophy of some sort. It is, then, an immensely practical subject, despite initial impressions. Like all disciplines it has its involved and complex terminology to baffle the laymen and at times keep us from meaningful discussion, but once we have cut through some of this we see that the foundational questions being addressed are plain and truly relevant to our everyday lives.

The problem of philosophy is essentially simple, and it evidently relates to the question of authority. The problem that philosophers have always sought to solve is that of the "one and the many" or the particular and the general. They ask, what is the universal principle or "unity" that makes the particulars of life (all life's objects of knowledge from atoms to antelopes) intelligible to us? Why is it that the world appears comprehensible to us? How is it that you and I relate to various objects and how are those objects related to each other? This is the problem of philosophy. In one sense what we all daily take for granted on the basis of some authority is what philosophy is seeking to examine.

However, we are in something of a catch-22 situation,

for in order to begin this process of examination legitimately, something (a principle, idea, or being) must be taken as self-evidencing or self-attesting. In other words, you have to start somewhere; in order to reason at all something must be taken for granted. To illustrate, if I say "X" is true and support this by showing it is verified by "Y," how do I know "Y" is true? I must then argue that "Y" is true because of another reason or reasons I can indicate in the abstract as "Z." But, then, how do I know "Z" is true? So the process goes on until we run out of abstract indicators in the alphabet. But obviously this cannot go on ad infinitum; we cannot argue in an endless chain, otherwise we could never establish our first premise "X." So in order to argue at all we necessarily presuppose the truth of something and that something must be taken as self-evidencing – a truth that need not (or cannot) appeal to anything else or beyond itself for verification.

When we boil it all down then, philosophy asks, what is the ultimate ground (basis) of the relationship between subjects (persons that know) and objects (things to be known)? How is it that we bring them to relate to each other? But in asking and examining what that ground is, we (the philosophers included) have already had to assume, wittingly or not, an ultimate ground of some kind – as we shall see, we have actually had to assume God, wittingly or not.

In all argument we must take for granted the authority of certain ideas/principles (presuppositions) as a starting point, in order to evaluate the assumed authority of another person's basic assumptions (i.e., theism and humanism respectively). Given this circumstance – that we cannot argue at all with these presuppositions – there is an inescapable circularity involved in argumentation.[1] So, the only way to proceed when assessing the truth or falsehood of a world view (network of presupposi-

---

1 Because in a valid argument the conclusion is seen to be entailed in the premises, premises are a form of conclusion. Thus, all meaningful premises are a conclusion of sorts which also requires an adequate foundation. We must therefore ask which world view can provide an adequate foundation for making meaningful statements.

tions) or theory of reality is to *work out its consequences*. Which world view provides an adequate foundation to make sense of human experience (logic, science, reason, morality, language, identity, dignity, etc.) and which, in contrast, destroys the very possibility of knowledge? In other words, which sort of circularity shows itself to be valid by making argument meaningful? Which view is internally coherent in terms of the presuppositions working and comporting with each other and which refutes itself with internal inconsistency? Put another way, which ultimate foundation allows human experience to be *what it appears to be?* Which "ground" can account for our universal belief in the validity of language, reason, logic, and science? Which does not make nonsense of our entire experience? In short, which theory of reality provides the preconditions necessary for the very notion of philosophy to be any more than meaningless verbiage?

Foundational Assumptions

To earth this a little in our minds let us highlight the four basic questions that we all must ask and seek to answer as human beings, as philosophers, in the context of any world view:

1. What is our origin?
2. What is the meaning and purpose of life?
3. What is our moral authority in ethics?
4. What is our final destiny?

All of our life is "religious" as we seek to deal with these fundamental questions. Which view of life can meaningfully deal with these great questions? Which provides an adequate basis for the intelligibility and meaningfulness of the questions themselves? Consequently, we see that to "love wisdom" is essentially "down to earth" and practical because what we believe with respect to these things will dramatically affect our behavior and life choices.

The Heart of the Matter

Now, as I have sought to show, my own culture, reflected in the bulk of my educational experience, offers its own response to these questions in the light of a non-Christian world view. Although secularism is by no means monolithic, and today imports and incorporates various ideas from Eastern philosophy, its numerous incarnations all share a common foundation or starting point. It is this starting point of *all* non-Christian thought that I now want to talk about.

As I remember my humanistic school days and my encounters with skeptics from all walks of life in my vocation since, the non-believers' essential starting point for thinking is the same. Invariably their arguments have already assumed, by definition, that the God and Father of the Lord Jesus Christ does not exist. I do not mean that they have all thought this through and are always intentionally starting with this assumption, but rather that their method of reasoning (assuming their own ultimacy and authority), having not begun with the authority of God's revelation but with some other independent intellectual starting point or criteria, demands the complete rejection of Christianity at the outset.

Most people take for granted the self-sufficiency and autonomy of their own experience. Most just assume that the reach of their logic, intellect, and knowledge of the facts is the final arbiter of truth, without ever asking what the very notion of logic, intellect, and fact, indeed knowledge of any kind, actually implies or demands. This frame of mind, when left unchallenged, is rarely prepared to consider seriously any fact or evidence that might undermine this assumed ultimacy and self-sufficiency. Consequently, it is this basic assumption which I must constantly bring to their attention and am seeking to bring to your attention now.

We have to be willing to get at the foundations of our experience. If we remain content to decorate the interior of the house of knowledge and pay no attention to the structure and foundation stones of that house, we will find that the dry rot of absurdity and the rising damp of unexamined assumptions are fatal to the structure.

Mission Impossible

I could, with little difficulty, present a great deal of careful argument and evidence for the truth of biblical Christianity, but the typical skeptic, drawing on popular hearsay, their secular schooling and the thinking of various scientists and philosophers, will generally suggest that no matter how compelling the evidence may appear to be to Christians, what we believe is not possible. What do they mean by this? The foundational doctrines of Christianity include the concepts of creation and providence, miracles and prophecy.[2] These foundational concepts, the skeptic will usually insist or at least infer, simply cannot by true. Modern "science" (science strictly means knowledge) has apparently proved the impossibility of the idea of creation – surely Darwin demonstrated this – and philosophy has shown the implausibility of the concept of the Christian creator God; their arguments and their system of reasoning demand that we cannot really know anything about God and all such talk about Him is gibberish.

As for miracles, miracles cannot happen and therefore they do not happen. What is capable of happening in an "open universe" is not a miracle, something affirmed by the Roman orator Cicero centuries ago. Thus, whoever or whatever Jesus was – doubtless a great human teacher and good man – He was not the Son of God, the Word (*logos* – thought of God) *made flesh,* the Creator and Sustainer of the universe.

As far as prophecy is concerned it is not possible to know the future in a chance-originating, chaotic universe. So although the Bible appears *to me* to predict in precise detail events occurring centuries later, this is not because a sovereign God who works out all things according to His eternal plan has revealed it. Such a God does not exist; therefore these

---

[2] I discuss all of these at some length in my earlier book *Searching for Truth.*

prophecies must be "postscripts" or I am just "reading in" things that are not objectively there. Alternatively, it is possible that these ancient peoples had an evolutionary adaptation giving special insight or psychic capability that we have lost. The one thing this prophecy *cannot* be is God's revelation of the future because that would mean human beings are not utterly free sovereigns, self-sufficient, self-sustaining, and self-interpreting.

The skeptic might permit the validity of my "experience" if I tell my story of knowing Jesus Christ and my conviction that through Christ I know God the Father. I will be allowed to speak in terms of feeling "aided" or "guided" in my life, believing I talk with God in prayer, explaining how He speaks to me through His Word. The experience itself is legitimate, but ascribing the "cause" of my experience to the God of the Bible, that is a problem. It may be that I eat too much rich cheese and that triggers my "religious experience." Perhaps I am one of a certain demographic that is psychologically susceptible to irrational religious feeling or bizarre epiphanies. One professor of philosophy I debated with admitted that some of his close friends in the academic world had become Christians. When asked whether it troubled him that he might be wrong about Christ, he confidently responded that he was not troubled. Why? Because he believed he could reduce their experience to a moment of crisis in life when they needed something to support them in a time of need and so turned to faith. In addition, he spoke of "memetic equilibrium," the notion that all religious ideas are merely viruses operating through an evolutionary process in the mind.[3] So, in the end, no matter what evidence may be presented, the "fact" or "experience" *cannot* be what it seems to what the Christian claims with respect to it.

On what basis is it impossible? Skeptics, often without even being conscious of it, rate what is plausible by their world view, essentially setting themselves up as God and making the

---

3   An idea borrowed from British scientist and popular humanist spokesman Richard Dawkins.

reach and preferences of their minds the measure of what is or is not possible and acceptable – an incredible metaphysical claim given our finite, limited circumstances. There is, in other words, a prior commitment in place to filter out all facts that point or lead to the God of the Bible. Cats or cows, horses or hedgehogs, sands below or stars above *cannot* be created by Jesus Christ but can only be what my independent reasoning says that they can be. Thus, human beings do not *discover* reality as God has created it, they must *legislate* for it, literally "creating it" out of their own minds in their image.

Choose your own authority!

The time has come, then, to challenge this human deification. What am I to make of the charge that my belief in Christ as God the Son and Lord of the universe is not credible, indeed, not possible?

Firstly, let me remind you of what we have noticed so far. I have tried to point out that, rather than starting with the presupposition of my own authority and independence, taking for granted (assuming as valid) "facts of experience and logic" without reference to God, I begin from a different position. Starting with the self-attesting revelation of God in Christ Jesus, I begin with the "fear of the Lord." In Scripture, the writer of Hebrews tells us that God must be presupposed if we are ever to know His mind and thereby have true understanding:

> Anyone who wants to come to him [God] *must believe* that there is a God and that he rewards those who sincerely seek him. (Hebrews 11:6, my emphasis)

Of which God does the writer of Hebrews speak? To whom is he referring? The apostle Paul tells us:

> Christ is the visible image of the invisible God. He existed before God made anything at all and is supreme

over all creation. Christ is the one through whom God created everything in heaven and earth. He made the things we can see and the things we can't see – kings, kingdoms, rulers, and authorities. Everything has been created through him and for him. He existed before everything else began, and he holds all creation together. (Colossians 1:15-17)

In such a case, because all wisdom and knowledge is then found in Christ, from the outset all my knowledge is "dependent" on God's knowledge. In other words, rather than presupposing the truth of "secular (this-worldly) principles" as my authority, I begin with Christ as my authority. To take a "middle ground" between these two is evidently impossible. One must begin with the authority of one or the other – Christ and the revelation of His Word or some other starting point. Consequently, we have seen there is no neutrality for any of us.

So my ultimate criterion, to understand all facts, is the authoritative revelation of God, as Scripture says, "In Your light we see light" (Psalm 36:9 NKJV). Or, to borrow the words of Augustine again, "I believe in order that I may understand." You also believe something in order that you may interpret and understand reality. But which belief leads to true understanding?

I have acknowledged that I believe God is truth and thereby the originator of all that is true. I have exposed my presuppositions to you. My knowledge is a receptive reconstruction of the absolute knowledge of God's mind, it is not original. The Christian should begin all interpretative activity with this principle consciously active. As the apostle Paul reminds us, "we have the mind of Christ" (1 Corinthians 2:16). Christ must be supreme in all of our thinking.

As a result I have affirmed that we will either live under the authority of God or by our own authority. In Matthew 7:29 it is noted that Jesus taught "as one who had real authority." He did not appeal to other people, to philosophers or scientists or scribes or even laws of reasoning to authenticate His message. How could He? To what source of expertise or authority could God the Son appeal except to His Father? As God He was self-authenticating and self-attesting, the very progenitor of being. He came with an absolute authority as the Creator and Sustainer of the universe. For those capable of seeing it, His authority was unmistakable. God does not and cannot appeal to human beings to authenticate His own message! Such a role reversal would be absurd. The Creator is not answerable to the creature, nor does He need the weight of human opinion to bolster or legitimize His claims.

In summary, then, this is the point at which we have now arrived. Autonomous people must appeal to other ordinary people for their authority. Jesus, however, says, "before Abraham was, I AM" (John 8:58 NKJV) and "I have come with my Father's authority" (John 5:43 GNB). The Christian appeals to Christ who speaks on His own authority (of the Godhead), the non-Christian must implicitly appeal to himself and his reasoning powers for his ultimate authority. I make my final appeal to the Creator God, His providence, and His revelation. Consistent non-Christian thought must finally appeal, philosophically, to chance as the sufficient, ultimate principle of the universe, the originator of humankind, and consequently of reason and logic also. Chance must be referred to as the final court of appeal in human thinking. It is, at bottom, the God of the Bible or chance. Jesus Christ or the void!

GIVE ME A CHANCE!

Let us continue by considering this crucial concept of chance. The providential God of the Bible and chance are totally antithetical hypotheses. Perhaps more precisely, the all-encompassing sovereign plan of God and chance are utterly incompatible and must be the ultimate antithesis between Christian and non-Christian thought. Scripture teaches us that there is nothing chaotic or random about the activity of God. He is the all-conditioning one, the ultimate sufficient cause[4] of all events, working all things according to the counsel of His will. These represent two contradictory world views. The first involves the personal God of the Bible freely choosing to create this universe with human beings intended as His vice-gerents, knowing and loving Him and finding their highest happiness in that relationship. In this meta-narrative the infinite self-contained (self-explanatory) Godhead brings all things into existence outside of Himself through special creation. God is back of everything. He is the ultimate cause, the final explanation, the necessary starting point in all predication[5] and our ultimate criterion for truth!

Now I argue that the only other view, and apparent alternative to this kind of God, posits, in the last analysis, the ultimacy of chance. Here an impersonal, content-less abstraction (idea that is not concrete – without particular examples) is the necessary starting point. Here chance, and not the personal

---

4   This means that God is not only the Creator, but the Sustainer of this world who animates all life. We do not find a sufficient cause for our lives in and of ourselves – we are not self-sustaining. The Apostle Paul tells us in Acts 17:28 (NKJV), *"For in Him we live and move and have our being."* The Bible teaches us that God rules providentially over all the affairs of human beings, according to His own secret will and wisdom. Although God is the sufficient and necessary ultimate cause of all events, He is not the instrumental cause of all events. For example, if you slapped someone around the face, you could not have done it without God's sustaining hand enabling you as the *sufficient* cause. However, strictly speaking, it was you and not God that slapped the person around the face. You were the *instrumental cause*. Because in Christian thought the Creator and creature are utterly distinct, we do not occupy a common scale of being. This means that what is said about God need not be "taken from" the attributes of people. For example: to say that God is the ultimate or primary cause who has an exhaustive plan for the universe does not mean that we must deny that people make free choices in this world of secondary causes.

5   Predication is the application of descriptive terms (predicates) in the world of objects and concepts. In other words, to describe anything at all, or have any warrant to believe that our description is valid, God must be presupposed.

triune God, stands behind everything.

GOD'S MYTHS AND MONSTERS

At the risk of passing over the matter too lightly, an appeal to other views of God, or "types" of god, at this point is abortive. All views of reality, whether conceived of as religious or secular, can initially be identified as falling into one of three categories. This is obviously a simplification as there are technically subgroups to these world views. However, the validity and coherence of any theory or hypothesis concerning reality is examined in the light of a network of presuppositions, or overarching frameworks that must take (broadly) one of the following three forms:

1. Theism – An infinitely perfect and personal God necessarily exists. God is distinct from the rest of creation that He called into existence and sustains by His power. Human beings have been made in God's image. Mind and matter are distinguishable entities as are body and soul. Morality is absolute and objective, grounded in the being and character of God.
2. Naturalism (materialism) – An absolute God, or any "supernatural" being, does not exist. All reality is spatio-temporal (part of the space-time world of matter and energy). Human beings are the product of mindless physical forces, a random collection of atoms. Mind is matter (if there is a mind at all). There is no soul or intellect that will outlive the body. Morality is subjective, a social and cultural convention. If there are gods of any kind they are finite and part of the universe (of nature).
3. Pantheism – All is one, one is all, and all is God! God is an impersonal oneness. All distinctions between God and the world or beings in the world are an illusion – there is no creator/creature distinction. Reality is a veil of illusion; human beings are not ultimately significant. All moral dis-

tinctions are dissolved. History has no end in view – it is cyclical not linear, involving re-births before joining an impersonal oneness.

Polytheism is not an ultimate world view as such. It is difficult to pin down as it has both a *pantheistic* and *naturalistic* expression. For example, in Hinduism, pantheism and polytheism go hand in hand with one impersonal Brahman plus 330 million gods manifesting the impersonal ultimate reality. But in its naturalistic expression, as in the ancient pagan religions of Babylonia, Greece, and Rome, the gods themselves were birthed by nature and so nature, not the gods, is ultimate. Their gods are finite (dependent or interdependent) in the universe, having sprung from mother-nature or a primordial watery chaos.

So polytheism is internally incoherent as all plurality presupposes a unity, i.e. a plurality – but of what? Furthermore, who or what arbitrates the disputes between the gods? And if there is a being that is ultimate from which the gods are derived, then polytheism proves theism!? Polytheism also requires an infinite series of *contingent events in time* – a philosophical absurdity. Regardless of the obvious incoherence noted, we see that polytheism is resolved either into naturalism or pantheism (or if applied inconsistently a deformed theism).

What relevance does all this have to the question of chance? Well, if you recall our discussion of the problem of philosophy, the one and the many, you will remember that we are asking what it is that makes reality a *"uni-*verse?" What, if anything, unites the particulars in our experience to make life intelligible? How do we relate as subjects to objects? And what can account for our belief in reason, logic, science, morality, language, and so forth? This fundamental question of philosophy is dealt with in a different way by these three world views.

One wonders!

Pantheism (all is God, God is all, so all is one) affirms the one (unity) but rejects the many (particulars); distinctions are an illusion. This means that real individuation (distinguishing between one thing and another) is actually impossible. Even basic logical distinctions are an illusion. This utterly destroys rationality and the possibility of knowledge (in principle). You might well ask the pantheist if pantheism as a belief system is true. If he says yes, you might then legitimately state it is also false, for no distinctions exist! If it is neither true nor false, then why discuss it at all? By having a discussion and disagreeing with the theist the pantheist contradicts himself. If he says, "That's Western logic," I would say, "Is Eastern logic different?" If so, then there are distinctions and again the pantheist defeats himself.

However, the point I want to make primarily is that pantheism resolves finally into the void of chance. God, in all the various permutations of pantheism, is identified with the world. If all reality is an *impersonal unity* where personality and individuality are annihilated, then you are left with an indistinguishable, undefinable, unintelligible void, without will, without intellect, without reason, or emotion. If there is a *universe* at all, our own individual minds are part of the illusion so I cannot even expose to others (there are no "others") the illusion that my mind is an illusion. Where there is no ultimate reasoning mind, chance, it seems, is the only abstraction left available to us.

Also, it is impossible to conceive of the pantheistic absolute unity. Because as soon as you try to describe it, it ceases to be a bare (absolute) unity! To affirm, for example, that all is God and I am God, whilst obviously being finite, means that God also must be finite – but how can He be both an absolute unity and finite?

There seems to me to be no adequate conception of *real* order (regularity) or *mind* that can be imposed upon the universe without recourse to personhood – even a computer must be programmed by a person. Whatever has "mind" and will" to "impose" any kind of order (especially moral order) must be *self*-aware, implying personhood. The moral order, for example, of reincarnation is not self-explanatory. Who or what governs the law of reincarnation? Why should one be reborn as a snail and another as a prince? What are the moral criteria for this cycle? In what is it grounded? It is simply incoherent to speak of an "impersonal" intelligence that is capable of *volitional action* imposing moral or structural order upon the universe.

In the end, pantheism is indistinguishable from atheism. It resolves into either a finite "god-ism" where indefinable divinity is relative to a reality of some sort (at the mercy of chance), or an unintelligible blank unity of nothingness, devoid of particulars, that neither knows nor is known. It is without personhood and so without a reasoning mind in any intelligible sense. Whatever actually can be meaningfully said about this monistic[6] world view (albeit self-contradictory), it appears to resolve reality into the only abstraction available if anything exists at all – chance!

Unnatural naturalism

Naturalism, on the other hand, affirms the many (particulars) and rejects the one (unity). The whole of the universe or reality as we know it collapses into an atomistic sea of matter in motion. Cornelius Van Til once illustrated this view by speaking of an infinite number of beads with no holes to string them together into a chain. So again we run aground on this question of the one and the many which is not solved by naturalism. We have no objective ground for distinguishing one thing from another. What makes simple things to differ? As I write this, I am sat on my chair, in my study. What makes me to differ from the chair – we are both matter in motion? Why do

---

6   Monism is the doctrine that all reality is one.

we live in a "uni-verse" not a "mono-verse?" Why am I different from a cloud of gas in outer space? What imposes order and structure and regularity upon entities so that there are individuals – persons, trees, varieties of grass, flowers, hippos and hedgehogs, insects and antelopes – why the variety and melody of nature rather than a deathly monotony?

Materialists strive to demonstrate (with their *immaterial theory*) that only matter exists[7] - all the time taking for granted the *immaterial* self-conscious "I" that is seeking to prove the "I" does not really exist. Again then, the god of materialism is chance. Matter and energy, time plus chance, we are told, is all there is. Thus, we are condemned to ignorance and the possibility of real knowledge (in principle) is destroyed. Of course, because neither pantheists nor naturalists are consistent with their own principles they do possess real knowledge of facts and experience. But what I am saying is that if they strictly applied their world views to their experience, all of life would be unintelligible. Both pantheism and naturalism end up in the realm of chance – or put another way, in the darkness of an unintelligible void of nothingness.

Christian theism (its theology, philosophy, and apologetics) does provide a basis and solution for the philosophical problem of the one and the many, revealing unity in diversity within the Godhead. The infinite, omniscient, and absolute mind of the eternal, personal community of the Trinity orders, defines, and differentiates one thing from another, providing a foundation for description, logic, morality, and reason.

---

7   The genetic revolution in microbiology has shown that information and the "matter" carrying that information are altogether different. DNA, for example, is a complex coded "language" of chemical letters written on molecules. A code is an intellectual and not a material entity. In building living organisms the same "raw material" (molecules) receive different instructions and so build different structures (types of cells). We are still only beginning to understand the complexity of this process.

Bare theism laid bare

The other *theistic* views, Judaism and Islam, are both related to Christianity but for different reasons. Jesus Christ claimed to be the Jewish Messiah promised to all nations and the fulfillment of the Old Testament law and prophecies. Christianity, embracing all of the Old Testament (believing in Jehovah), claims therefore to be the seamless and plainly foretold continuation of God's progressive revelation through the Jewish people, in Christ God's Son, the promised one. The ancient Jewish people, kings, prophets, and priests knew God by faith in the promises concerning the Savior (Messiah) who would come. All the revelation they received was designed to teach them their need for faith in the Christ, the sacrificial Lamb of God, and the unbreakable promises of God. Those Jews who rejected Jesus as such continued the practice of Judaism. Many are still looking and hoping for their Messiah two thousand years on. The Jewish writers of the New Testament teach that many Jewish people have thus failed to recognize the Messiah; at root this is due to their failure to recognize the triune nature of God as seen in Jesus' discussions with Jewish teachers in the gospels.

Islam, founded over six hundred years after Christ, rests on the supposed angelic revelations of the military and political figure Mohammed. Though claiming a unity with and dependence upon the authority of the Bible, as God's "final" prophet, Mohammed's "revelations" plainly contradict and greatly distort the actual history and doctrines of the Scriptures (both Old and New Testaments). His disjointed prophetic *modifications* maul Scripture beyond recognition to the point where they deny that men and women need a savior or that Christ was the Son of God (not to mention serious factual, historical, and geographical errors). This contradiction and countless others are "reconciled" by the incredible claim that the Bible has been grossly corrupted, but no literary evidence of any credible kind has ever been shown by historical scholarship and textual criticism, especially over the past seventy years. Hence some scholars have referred to Islam as the last great Christian heresy.[8]

Both of these world religions (Judaism and Islam) hold a strict monadic[9] view of God. Philosophically this reduces God again to a *bare unity* (without particulars), necessarily devoid of distinction in His being and consequently not transcendent (defined by, rather than above or distinct from His creation). It appears impossible to conceive of a monadic god as anything more than an infinite, impersonal block of ice. Such a god does not provide a solution to the problem of the "one and the many" (being a bare oneness). Only in the triune God of Christianity is there unity in diversity (three united in one) that can account for the unity in diversity that we see in the universe and natural order.

The conundrum

Is reality one or many? Unable to agree, the philosophers are divided. But Christian theism sees this question as a faulty dilemma. Reality is not one or the other but both – to be intelligible it must be. The Trinity alone can provide an equal ultimacy of the general (one) and particular (many) and so avoid the destructive futility of non-Christian thought. Only here does the general (unity) not destroy the intelligibility (or

---

8   A heresy is a departure from Christian orthodoxy. Heresies tend to have a semblance of truth but distort the Bible and Christian truth at crucial points. They invariably begin with an individual claiming fresh revelation or insight that supposedly modifies or adds to the revelation of Christ. Well-known modern examples include Mormonism, Jehovah's Witnesses, and I would include Islam. An excellent collation of the textual and historical evidences for the authenticity of Scripture can be found in Josh McDowell's *The New Evidence that Demands a Verdict* (Nashville: Thomas Nelson, 1999).

9   A monadic view of God holds that He exists as a bare unity, as a singularity, a solitary being. In this view of God there is no plurality (distinction of person in the Godhead) and therefore no "transcendence" intrinsic to God's being.

existence) of the particulars and vice versa (as in naturalism and pantheism). Why? Because in the Trinity all three members (persons) are equally ultimate. The Father, Son, and Holy Spirit all constitute the Godhead – one God, unity in diversity, an eternal community of personal relationship. It is here that knowledge can begin (subject and object distinction) and predication (describing or stating truth about anything) becomes meaningful. Only here does all reality avoid collapsing into one undifferentiated void, making all rational thinking impossible.

Here in the biblical doctrine of the Trinity – which is proved ultimately in the person of Christ – the age-old problem of philosophy is finally brought to rest. Jesus Christ is the answer to the problem of philosophy. He has come to save the human person and enterprise entirely, from sin and futility, including futile science and philosophy. He has come to redeem it all, and to save us all from useless and worthless thoughts, giving us a true science and philosophy. We cannot compartmentalize life and say that Christ can save us spiritually or ethically but has nothing to do with history, philosophy, or science. Christ redeems the soul, the body, and the mind – He transforms our minds. All these aspects of the human person are interrelated and inseparable: He cannot save one without saving the other. Christ's Lordship extends over all of reality; only in this way does He answer the problem of godless philosophy. The unity in diversity that we see in the universe is rooted in Christ Jesus the Creator, Savior, and Sustainer of it all. It is the infinite mind of the "Word" (Christ the thought of God) that creates, defines, differentiates, describes, unites, and upholds all things; the one who knows Himself (the other persons of the Godhead) as well as His creation exhaustively. It is He alone who can tell us what reality is. We are called to think His thoughts after Him.

It is important to note, in the light of the Trinity, that in the other theistic views God must become *dependent* upon the world for character and content to His being – thereby ceasing to be transcendent and thus ceasing to be God. For example, who was Allah loving before he created the world? To whom or to what was he related to display any virtue? Prior to creation, how could such a god have any moral character or even know himself – given that there is no "not-self," no possibility of distinction? The concept of a pure mind without distinction, where there is nothing and nobody to know, given the relational nature of all knowledge (which needs a subject and object) requiring a medium of communication, is totally incoherent. Such a god is reduced to an "*it,*" the god of the ancient Greeks, an abstract oneness about which nothing can be said. *It* neither knows nor is known. *It* cannot be personal or relational. Thus again, such a god becomes contingent (not absolute), interrelated to the universe and subject to chance, caught in a reality in which *it* is an impersonal, necessary cause (an impersonal cause that could not help causing an effect, so in a sense the effect is the cause of the cause) neither free nor controlling anything, and so like human beings is made *relative* to the world. So I affirm that chance *must reign* in any view where the absolute, triune, self-contained God of the Bible is not presupposed.

To be or not to be?

Some of the last section is admittedly difficult to take in (especially if you have not been exposed to some of the philosophical terminology before) and is by far the hardest section of this book. I have done my best to unpack complex thoughts as briefly, simply, and clearly as my ability will allow. It was by no means an exhaustive treatment, but it indicates the main conceptual problems in the other world views and the essential conceptual starting point of the Christian world view.

The main point to remember is essentially this, that a consideration of the Trinity is utterly central to a Christian understanding of philosophy as derived from Scripture and in fact *essential* for understanding how we have any knowledge at all. I would encourage you to reflect deeply on the points made above if you have had some difficulty accepting the doctrine of the Trinity or are wrestling with unitarian notions of god, or pantheistic and new age theosophies.

We come at last to the slippery, enigmatic, and abstract notion of chance. I have suggested, in all of my discussion above, that in the final analysis there are only two *ultimate* world views (the three reduce to two): a version of pagan impersonalism or the God of the Bible; Christian theism or chance! Chance involves the ideas of randomness, unpredictability, and chaos. To invoke *natural laws* at this point does us no good because those so-called "laws" find their "origin" in chance, consequently natural laws are not ultimate for we must ask what is *natural* and what are *laws – what is our warrant for accepting them?* In a universe where chance is ultimate, these abstract laws might change at any moment! The well-established laws of thermodynamics (dealing with the movement and characteristics of energy) or the law of gravitation would have to be seen as nothing more than "statistical anomalies" in the chaos. They are pure abstractions because in principle, in a chance universe, "prescription" (stating what will happen) is impossible. In other words, to speak of the "laws of chance" is simply a contradiction in terms.

Of necessity then, all impersonalistic world views must hold to an *evolutionary view* of the entire universe, including natural "laws" (that are not laws), whether evolving eternally in absurd endless cycles or springing from nothing and so creating itself! This view goes all the way back in recorded history to the ancient Babylonians who believed the gods themselves evolved from a primeval watery chaos. Thus, every view but the Judeo-Christian view must invoke evolutionism of some kind. This evolving universe may or may not contain a finite god (or gods), who like men and women is caught in the continuum of reality where chance operates over and above them; here anything is possible, even the evolution of a god. Whatever the case may be or whatever subtle permutation may be drawn from these ideas, at bottom chance must be ultimate *if* the universe is governed and directed by no person, no will, no ultimate intelligent being, no triune God of Scripture. The universe is just there; it just is, leaving *chance* as the only remaining "explanation" or governing principle available.

Thus, in the popular secular thought of the West all is indeed interpreted as a *"random collocation of atoms,"* as Bertrand Russell once put it. Being is all the same stuff – it is just arranged differently by chance. Existence is all on one level and subject to pure possibility. If there is any god, he is also a prisoner of the continuum. But don't be fooled, this is *not* a modern idea. It is another tributary from a stream in ancient Greek thought known as atomism. A number of noted Greek thinkers such as Democritus and Epicurus taught a naturalistic doctrine of "chance" in a universe of eternal matter (atoms) over 2,000 years ago. Their modern counterparts have brought no essential modification – just variations on a theme.

SLIM CHANCE

But have you ever asked yourself the question, what is chance? It is not a power, a force, a substance, or even energy. In fact, it isn't anything substantive at all. It is not a concrete idea but an empty abstract notion. It is just a word. A word we use to describe the collision of certain events that we did not directly cause or purpose to happen. We therefore say that a given thing occurred by chance. It is descriptive only of our inability to know, predict, and interpret reality exhaustively. It is a concept we relate closely to that of probability. If I toss a coin, we say there is a *chance* that it will land heads up. Let us say that it does indeed land heads up. Did *chance* have anything to do with the outcome? Of course not. Chance isn't anything, it simply identifies my ignorance. I am in a hopeless epistemic position to judge the outcome of a tossed coin. I do not know what forces are acting upon it precisely as I flip it. I do not know exactly how many times it will turn over in the air or the resistance it will encounter. Consequently, precise prediction is impossible for me as *all the facts were not in:* therefore we call it *chance.*

I am finite, neither self-sustaining nor self-sufficient. I have only a tiny proportion of the facts at my disposal. I neither created, control, nor sustain this universe, therefore I am hopelessly placed to "see through" reality, never mind legislate what it is or must be. It is only to God, who has created and controls all things, that all the facts are known fully. Nothing escapes Him or is unknown to Him, and therefore only He knows all exhaustively and can predict and interpret every event in this universe. So we see unequivocally that the God of the Bible and chance are opposite explanations. Either a personal God in a personal universe (atmosphere) has a sovereign control and exhaustive plan for this world or the empty notion of impersonal chance governs reality.

Reason in the balance

Where then does a chance universe leave us? What are the consequences which flow from this notion? It is often admitted that in a universe where chance is ultimate, ultimate irrationality is the outcome; there can be no objective or absolute truth. In fact, this conclusion is inescapable, for in such a world even the activity of my brain is chaotic and random. The doctrine of chance means that events can and do happen without a predictable, knowable rational cause. Often when I ask someone who believes that the big bang hypothesis can explain everything, how this random explosion originated, they tell me it was by chance – that is, for no reason that they know, it just happened. This response obviously sidesteps a causal argument which shows that if we are to retain causation as a meaningful (not psychological) concept in science, every contingent event requires an efficient and sufficient cause to make it intelligible. For the universe, we are told, we do not have one. The causal argument is considered invalid. Apparently, every finite, space-time event does not need a sufficient cause. Apparently, something can create itself and come from nothing. I also often remind people who hold this view that speaking of chance as an agent in the *collision* of entities (even though, as we have seen, chance is not an agent) does not tell us anything about the origin of the entities (events) themselves. The notion of chance presupposes entities that might collide.

The search for a cause can also be expressed as the search for a reason. All questions about the cause of an event are asking about the *reason for* an event. Consequently, if something happens by chance in the sense meant by opponents of Christianity (i.e. randomness) it is happening without an ultimate reason. Clearly nothing can be said about chaos except that it is chaos – nothing can be predicated of chaos, it just is – chaos is chaos! This is what undergirds the chance world view. Thus, the world must be *ultimately irrational,* or *without reason.* Chaos has no reason and does not speak! Thus, the ultimacy of chance means the ultimacy of irrationality. The nature of reality itself is irrationality.

What then can be meaningfully said about reality? What can be meaningfully said about anything at all? How can anyone even form a *rational* argument about the irrationality of the universe? How can anyone say that God cannot possibly exist, or that Christ is not God or that the Bible cannot be true, when nothing they have said has a rational foundation and thereby any meaning? In fact, everyone is left in the position where all meaningful language and discourse is annihilated. It is therefore legitimate for the Christian apologist to say that forming an argument against the divinity of Christ and the truth of the Bible involves the debater unwittingly having to presuppose the divinity of Christ to make his argument meaningful. To deny the Christian God is as nonsensical as two men shouting at each other in an argument about whether sound exists. Cornelius Van Til expressed it in a similar way, suggesting that to deny God and His existence is like a small child sat on her father's knee and slapping him around the face. The child can only slap her father because the father supports her and holds her up to a sufficient height! Antitheism presupposes theism, as Van Til once succinctly put it.

Finally, consider whether we can even talk about what is probable or not – the very heart of the scientific method. Chaos and chance cannot have any meaningful connection with the idea of probability. If the universe is chaotic and irrational, probability can never be calculated or considered a meaningful concept. Asking what is probable or not in such a universe is absurd for nothing can be either probable or improbable where chance reigns. But Christ Jesus reigns and rules over all things and so we can meaningfully speak of probability. The apostle Paul writes in Colossians 1:15-17:

> Christ is the visible image of the invisible God. He existed before God made anything at all and is supreme over all creation. Christ is the one through whom God created everything in heaven and earth . . . Everything has been created through him and for him. He existed before everything else began, and he holds all creation together.

Only on the foundation of the Christ of Scripture, who gives order, structure, and consistency to the universe, holding all things together, can the idea of probability have any meaning for us. Science is possible, probability is meaningful, only because God has promised in His Word that there will be consistency and regularity in nature, that the future will be like the past: the sun will rise, the seasons will change, until Christ returns.

As a consequence, in the world of chance, useful knowledge itself becomes impossible. Even to distinguish one fact from another in the process of *differentiation* becomes impossible, given that the arrangement of all the facts is inherently random and always in flux. Naturally, then, a coherent view of reality based on learning of any kind becomes an absurd idea, an empty dream. Human beings are condemned to a life of ignorance and skepticism, always uncertain of everything, though not certain why they should be uncertain!

The ramifications of this for all the sciences should now be very clear to you – we cannot even begin to do science upon the principles of impersonalism and chance! The universe is irrational, so the scientific project becomes as useful as a cat-flap in an elephant house. The sciences require an opposite view, a Christian theistic view, before they have any plausible foundation. Therefore, it should not surprise us when we find modern science being birthed and developed in "Christendom" during and after the sixteenth-century Protestant Reformation and renaissance involving many scientists who were Christian theists that believed the Bible (thought I doubt most of us were taught this in school). To name just a few that might surprise you, they include such legendary names as Sir Isaac Newton (1642-1727), Johannes Kepler (1571-1630), Blaise Pascal (1623-1662), Francis Bacon (1561-1626), Robert Boyle (1627-1691), Carl Linnaeus (1707-1778), Georges Cuvier (1769-1832), Charles Babbage (1791-1871), Michael Faraday (1791-1867), Louis Pasteur (1822-1895), Gregor Mendel (1822-1884), Sir Joseph Lister (1827-1912), James Clerk Maxwell (1831-1879), Sir Ambrose Fleming (1849-1945), James Prescott Joule (1818-1889), and various other fathers of the sciences through several hundred years. Isaac Newton said, "I have a fundamental belief in the Bible as the Word of God."[10] He also wrote: "Atheism is so senseless. When I look at the solar system, I see the earth at the right distance from the sun to receive the proper amounts of heat and light. *This did not happen by chance.*"[11] Johannes Kepler with similar sentiment wrote: "now I see how God is, by my endeavors glorified in astronomy, for 'the heavens declare the glory of God.'"[12]

James Prescott Joule, the nineteenth-century English

---

10   Cited by Ann Lamont in 21 *Great Scientists Who Believed the Bible* (Brisbane: Creation Science Foundation., 2000), 37.

11   *Ibid.*, 37 (my italics).

12   *Ibid.*, 15.

scientist, was a very important scientific figure and member of the prestigious Royal Society. Discovering what has come to be called Joule's Law he made vital contributions to our understanding of physics, especially in the field of thermodynamics – in fact, he is recognized as the main founder of thermodynamic theory, demonstrating its validity from data collected in his experiments. His principle of energy conservation became the basis for the *first law* of thermodynamics, undoubtedly one of the most important theories in the history of scientific endeavor. Joule wrote: "*Order* is manifestly maintained in the universe . . . the entire machinery, complicated as it is, works smoothly and harmoniously . . . the whole being governed by the *sovereign will of God.*"[13] He also noted: "It is evident that an acquaintance with *natural laws* means no less than an acquaintance with the *mind of God* therein expressed."[14]

I affirm that chance as a dogma is antithetical to science. It is *impossible* that a successful scientific method could have arisen from a secular world view consistently applied. The irony is that secularism must "borrow" the tool of reason (among other things) from Christianity in order to carry out the task of propagating secularism.

THE RAFT OF REASON ON A SEA OF CONFUSION

The resulting dilemma of non-Christian thought can be illustrated by the following picture. In principle, in this world, the unbelieving person, whom we will call Mr Autonomy (self-law), discovers he is (or at least believes himself to be) in an ocean of pure possibility. Inexplicably he finds himself "aboard" a structure of norms (of logic, reason, and language hardware), a vessel which we will call the "raft of reason." Adrift on this vessel, with no land in sight, he is inescapably aware of a relationship between the particulars (or facts) all around him and the given structure of norms in his mind that

---

13 *Ibid.*, 133 (my italics).
14 *Ibid.*, 133 (my italics).

make the "knowing" process possible.

Looking up at the night sky he sees the stars and realizes, like the ancient mariners, that they can provide a transcendent and ultimate point of reference to make navigation of the vessel of reason possible. However, instead of acknowledging and taking seriously the *revelation* provided in the heavens (that is inescapably correlated to the revelation of norms in his use of logic and reason) for safe and meaningful navigation, he asserts his utter independence and arbitrarily decides that he is self-sufficient. He tells himself that "man is the measure of all things," that he alone will be the final reference point in navigating the ocean of particulars – he must be the final criterion for truth and predication. So Mr Autonomy sets sail.

Unfortunately, Mr Autonomy has foolishly assumed an *authority* that can lead him nowhere! Given that he (as his own final point of reference) is aboard the vessel of reason, he moves wherever the wind of thought may take him. Mr Autonomy aimlessly drifts on through the ocean of particulars all around him utterly lost. He has no idea *where* he is, he only knows *that* he is. All his attempts at plotting a route and navigating the vessel of reason fail dismally because where the vessel moves, he moves also (Mr Autonomy is the reference point – they have become synonymous). Though he may travel a great distance across the ocean, he might just as well have traveled nowhere, because he does not know which point he has traveled from or which point he is traveling to – and the ocean all around him looks the same in every direction. He has no idea where he has been or where he is going. Every effort Mr Autonomy makes to ascertain his position – obtain real knowledge in the ocean of particulars and differentiate between locations – is doomed to failure because he is everywhere and nowhere in relation to himself.

Imagine, if the shoreline moved with a ship as it sailed out of dock, how could you know whether you had left or moved at all? The point of reference is lost. Consequently, so long as Mr Autonomy ignores the objective *revelation* in the heavens that provide a *transcendent* point of reference, being the precondition of successful navigation, he can do nothing more than devise abstract shipping routes and relate them to subjective and arbitrarily placed buoys he might drop in the water. His own mind must literally map and "invent" reality on an arbitrary basis – as a result all his knowledge has a random source. Mr Autonomy's reason becomes as useless as an escalator in outer space. Being everywhere and nowhere in relation to himself on an ocean of particulars, east or west, north or south, nautical miles traveled (or not traveled) or speed in knots, cannot be determined, one fact cannot be differentiated from another!

    If we will not be content to discover what reality is by relating everything back to the transcendent God of creation, thinking His thoughts after Him, guided by His clear revelation, in His Word and in His world, (special and general revelation), we must invent an illusory reality for ourselves, elevating our position to that of god and then live with the futility and vanity of the thinking I have described. We must choose between the safe and meaningful ark of God's truth or being cut adrift on the ocean of despair, aboard the raft of our own delusions.

DEFINE AND EXPLAIN THESE WORDS AND PHRASES:

1. Philosophy
2. Chance

ANSWER THE FOLLOWING QUESTIONS:

1. What is chance? Why does Joe say that the God of the Bible and chance are opposite explanations? (p. 126-127)
2. What religions does Joe describe as 'bare theism'? What does this term mean? What is the key difference between bare theism and Christianity?
3. What is the difference between an individual 'religious experience' caused by natural events like eating too much cheese, and an experience caused by the God of the Bible?
4. Do you agree with Joe's claim that the Trinity is essential for understanding how we can have any knowledge at all? Why or why not?

Chapter 8
Firm Foundations

"Anyone who listens to My teaching and obeys Me is wise, like a person who builds a house on solid rock. Though the rain comes in torrents and the floodwaters rise and the winds beat against that house, it won't collapse, because it is built on rock. But anyone who hears My teaching and ignores it is foolish, like a person who builds a house in sand. When the rains and floods come and the winds beat against that house, it will fall with a mighty crash."

Matthew 7:24-27

"The Holy Scripture is to me, and always will be, the constant guide of my assent; and I will always hearken to it, as containing the infallible truth relating to things of highest concernment . . . Where I want the evidence of things, there yet is ground enough for me to believe, because God has said it; and I will presently condemn and quit any opinion of mine, as soon as I am shown that it is contrary to any revelation of the Holy Scripture."

- John Locke

House of sand or rock?

Like everybody else I have had to choose which foundation I am going to build my life upon. Who or what can provide a stable foundation for my thinking, feeling, acting, and living as a man? This question always brings me back to this final dichotomy between Christian and non-Christian thought. We have admitted the presuppositions which lie behind each argument, for and against Christianity; this is crucial if we are to make any headway in our understanding. Where we begin in our thinking, our method of argument and our conclusions are all "involved" in each other. Our premises *are* a form of conclusion, which is why in any valid argument our conclusions should follow our premises. So we see that our conclusions in life revolve around the starting point[1] of our thought, our ultimate criteria for truth (a conclusion that determines what other conclusions we will reach), the very foundation of all our thought! Upon which foundation will you build?

    I have tried to outline which view makes human experience intelligible and which does not. Only one set of presuppositions provides a rational warrant for proving anything at all, only one world view makes sense of our most basic practical assumptions in life. My contention is that only Christian presuppositions that build upon Christ and His Word provide a platform for the *house of human knowledge* to be what it actually is in our experience. I have been arguing *by implication* that the necessary foundation or precondition of the knowledge we readily assume and possess, is biblical Christianity and that all other accounts destroy the very possibility of human knowing – our accepted use of reason as a tool of knowing, for

---

1   Our "starting point" is not necessarily a reference to the usual temporal order of our thoughts as though we consciously begin all our thinking with a given assumption. It refers specifically to the platform upon which our thought is or must be built when we carefully analyze it. Because most of us are inconsistent and lazy in our thinking, we have often failed to see our intellectual starting point or understand its ramifications.

example, implies the truth of Christianity.[2]

So I have sought to turn the complaint of the skeptic upon its head as I share the message of Christ. The skeptic has often told me my faith in Christ demands belief in the impossible. I have to respond by asserting that any view *other than* one built upon Christ, the Creator and Redeemer of this world, is what constitutes the impossible; that even for one to argue for the impossibility of my view involves taking the truth of it for granted, if the skeptic would just be consistent with his or her own principles.

So I would encourage you at this stage to ask yourself again, what are your laws and facts? What is your final point of reference, the platform for your thinking? Do you stand with those who say Christianity is impossible or are you beginning to see things from the "other side?"

Proof positive!

The essence, then, of the Christian argument really resolves all the so-called proofs for Christian theism into one. I argue, with many other Christian apologists, that unless the God of the Bible, the Creator and Controller of the universe, is presupposed as the foundation of human experience, our experience operates in an unintelligible void. To me this "proof" (outlined in the last chapter) is utterly convincing and is sufficient to show the fatal inadequacy and futility of all other world views. The void or God – that is our choice! Of course, I am not suggesting that people always consciously see this antithesis as they reflect on their experience. As I have said, non-believers must "borrow rocks" from the foundation of the

---

2   Reason and logic as tools do not supply the truths or facts concerning reality (premises); rather as part of our God-given nature, they are instruments we use to reach true conclusions from our premises. But to reach true conclusions those premises must be supplied by God's revelation, both natural (in the world and ourselves) and special (in Scripture). If we get our premises from the vain imaginations of people we cannot reach true conclusions.

Christian world view in order to shore up the sandy foundation beneath their house of knowledge. This is often done quite unconsciously. But, in principle, were they consistent with their avowed beliefs, they would be living and building life in an unintelligible infinite emptiness, lacking a foundation to construct or critique any world view!

I believe this proof constitutes a rational certainty, even if it does not persuade everybody psychologically. An argument may be rationally certain and at the same time, for a number of reasons (some of which we have discussed), be "unconvincing" to certain minds and hearts. I believe in Jesus Christ, in part because all contrary views show themselves to be impossible by implication. As so many unwittingly do today, to apply abstract laws (chance originating ideas) to irrational facts (chaotic particulars) is to chase the wind, as Scripture states concerning all thought under the sun that does not put God first: "'Everything is meaningless,' says the Teacher, 'utterly meaningless'" (Ecclesiastes 1:2).

The argument can be arranged in simple logical order in the form of a syllogism. I will put it to you in both a positive and negative form. First, put negatively:

1. If God does not exist, the world is unintelligible
2. God does not exist
3. Conclusion: Therefore the world is unintelligible.

But, as we have noted and Einstein acknowledged (and you certainly don't need to be an Einstein to see it), the world *is* intelligible to us. The conclusion is therefore false and, consequently, premise two must be false. Now to put it in the positive form:

1. If the world is intelligible, God exists
2. The world is intelligible
3. Conclusion: Therefore God exists.

So a truly consistent Christian argument seeks to show that reality is unintelligible apart from God at every level: causal (the relationship between cause and effect), axiological (our sense of moral obligation (ethics) and aesthetic beauty), ontological (understanding and distinguishing being of every kind), and teleological (the purpose and design we see in nature). None of these things can be what they appear to be without God; none of them make any sense without Him. In the absence of a faith commitment to God and His Word, would-be autonomous human reasoning leads to the death of rationality and meaning.

As a result, poor autonomous human beings are in a terrible state, caught in a whirlpool from which they cannot escape. They cannot be certain about anything in this "open universe" (chance); they do not have all the facts at their disposal and never will, as an infinite number of things are beyond them, so they can never be sure they have the right interpretation of those facts. They cannot even be sure that their memory is reliable concerning past observation or experience: there is no *basis* for trusting their memory or their reason. In fact, autonomous human beings cannot even know that they are the same person they were last week, last year, or the last decade. In their chance world the concept of personal identity is incoherent. When all reality is in flux you never put your foot in the same river twice, as the pre-Socratic Greek philosopher Heraclitus famously said: they cannot know that they are the person they see in pictures from the past. In what sense are *randomly coalescing atoms* and *bundles of sensation* individual persons from one moment to the next? They *must* go on believing that the universe is irrational in an ultimate sense, whilst insisting on the validity of their reasoning power and *rational* logic to argue for the *irrationality* of reality. They deny Christian theism, claiming that their reason cannot accept it, whilst implicitly affirming that they have no foundation to do *any* reasoning at all! Yes, autonomous skeptics must be both totally certain (about their rationality) and absolutely uncertain about everything both at the same time, a psychological impossibility! As Van Til has shown us, they must be rationalists and irrationalists both at the same time, asserting their rational independence (a certain denial of Christianity) whilst affirming the ultimate irrational nature of all reality.

So from the fortress built upon the rock that is Christ I am able to challenge those seeking to break down the gates and storm the keep of biblical revelation by asking them how the world is intelligible and meaningful when built upon their own assumptions. It becomes clear that, in order to throw stones at the fortress gates, the assailant must himself stand on the rock foundation upon which the fortress is built! Thus, I believe it is skepticism that must retreat! It is easy for a person to sit and doubt or deny anything and everything, appearing humble and wise as they do it, thinking that in so doing they have intelligently affirmed nothing - but nothing could be further from the truth. Every denial is a significant affirmation of a faith position resting in a void. So I would encourage you to have the courage to re-examine your foundations. Let us all face ourselves with integrity.

Nobody's perfect

I have sought to obey Christ and build my life upon the rock, and I can feel the stability of that foundation every day. This does not mean I have never been wrong or made significant mistakes; on the contrary, I am as fallible as any person. Even as a Christian apologist I have, at times, adopted views and practices that I have later seen to have been misguided and wrongheaded, albeit well-intentioned. Like John Locke (quoted at the beginning of the chapter) I am ready to "quit" any belief that I am shown is contrary to the authoritative revelation of God. God is truth: if I conflict with Him I need to revisit my faulty interpretations of God's Word or God's world. I want my life built upon the rock which is the Word of Christ, not the sand of my own speculations.

The God I worship, however, is perfect, speaking with absolute authority as He knows, controls, and interprets all the facts – He is, therefore, an able teacher! He is my authoritative guide. It is in Him that possibility finds its meaning. He has revealed Himself clearly in His creation and that revelation is rightly interpreted by *supernatural thought communication* in the Scriptures. Together, Christ's witness in the created world and His Word form a unified whole, each supporting, interpreting, and presupposing the other. It is only in the light of His revelation of Himself both naturally and supernaturally that anything makes any sense to me at all.

Unity and glory

Is it possible that somewhere, deep inside your own heart, you already recognize the things I have been saying are true? That as you have been reading this, even amid the rigor of thought, something in your soul has stirred and acknowledged what is plain to those who seek God with integrity? Is it possible you are conscious that there is no real unity in your life, nothing that unites it all together making sense of the things you value? Perhaps you have striven for a long time to provide your own sense of unity through money or entertainment or sex or a career or even in family and friends, but a satisfying unity and accompanying rest still elude you.

Through no ingenuity of my own I have an ever-present unity in my experience, a unity I have sought to share here in aspects of my story, a unity provided by the worship of the God I love. It is Christ as God's Son who is my unity making sense of my work, my marriage, my leisure, my children, my past, present, and future. This unity holds true for the good and bad times that we all experience in life; in happiness and in grief, in my times of joy as well as times of despondency. In the lives of my immediate family, Christ has brought unity of meaning and purpose even in times of terrible loss. Indeed, the unity in life that Christ brings is never more evident than in those moments I have stood by the graves of my grandparents, or by the grave of my brother who died in infancy. In fact, grief over loss and loved ones has no meaning or significance – it is rendered unintelligible – unless Christ is who He claims to be.

Only the Christian world view can give a meaningful account of grief and the human condition. If you and I are just "matter in motion," why grieve when another random assortment of bio-chemical material has lost vital functions – what is the meaning of a funeral? Loss and grief, even tragedy itself, make no sense in a universe of "selfish genes" and "random replication." Why is it that my grandparents, whom I loved (love itself, from the secular humanist perspective, is only random chemical reactions), have more dignity and value to me than rats living in a sewer or a hive of bees? None of us, except those who are dishonest with themselves or out of touch with their own humanity, would deny that a human being has more intrinsic worth than an insect. So what warrants this truly human conviction? What can make sense of my grief or the need for a funeral?

Unbelieving philosophy simply cannot offer a rational account of human dignity or the intrinsic value of a person. In order to make sense of any of our experiences as human beings, atheists and skeptics must borrow from Christian theism, revealing the total lack of systematic cogency in the presuppositions of unbelievers; they simply do not comport. The question of unity in our experience once again exposes the fatal inadequacy of non-Christian thought – it cannot be lived out consistently or sustained in principle. Secularism, upon its own principles, is reduced to irrational and arbitrary superstition when assuming human value and dignity (i.e. wanting a formal funeral) yet dresses itself up as cold rationality! When simply asked to give account of (justify) the most basic of our human assumptions, beliefs, and experiences non-Christian thought is left utterly bewildered.

The Christian unity of which I speak is not one that I

have arrived at by my own intellectual independence and ingenuity. I do not share what I have to brag or because I consider my intellectual powers sufficient to see through reality. On the contrary there are skeptical minds with a higher IQ than I possess who are not Christians and there are Christians equally superior who are not skeptics. That is not the issue. You can comprehend Einstein's theories of relativity and still be a fool, and you can be illiterate yet wiser than most, for the gap between the learned and the unlearned is very small, indeed, when it comes to the question of our foundations. We can only properly explore the relationships between those things that we can apprehend. Thus, the clear-sighted illiterate man has the advantage over the Harvard professor who is blind, when it comes to star gazing. All the brain power on earth is of no use if we are blind to that which is real.

But having been granted spiritual sight by the grace of God, I have the unity of a worshiper. As a finite replica, a creature, it is my Creator who gives significance and purpose to all of my activities. All that I see and discover with the judicious use of my mind refers me back to the original unity that is in the providential plan of the triune God. I do not need to replace God and invent a unity; I only need to worship and reflect His.

Eric Liddell, the early twentieth-century Olympian who won the 400 meters final in 1924, was a Christian and a missionary to China. In fact, he died in China shortly after the Second World War. He was a brilliant athlete and a unique man of principle and self-sacrifice. The biographical film Chariots of Fire depicts this with a scene between him and his sister Jenny who wondered whether his athletics would get in the way of his service for God in China. He responded to her, "Jenny, God has made me for a purpose, for China, but he has also made me fast and when I run, I feel his pleasure."[3] That is Christianity: finding unity in all the diverse activities of life in the worship, pleasure, and plan of God. That is how

3   *Chariots of Fire*. Directed by Hugh Hudson. London: Enigma Productions, 1981.

you can win or lose, rejoice or mourn, be rich or poor, sick or healthy, and be satisfied. That is how one can find a consistency worshipping God as a banker, a baker, or a candlestick maker, playing golf, or preaching the message of Christ in Outer Mongolia. It is Christ alone who unites and makes sense of it all, as the apostle Paul writes, "Therefore, whether you eat or drink, or whatever you do, do all to the glory of God" (1 Corinthians 10:31 NKJV).

Holding the hand of God

This unity I experience does not mean I have everything worked out. I don't know why some things happen or why other things do not. I see beauty in life and ugliness, joy and sadness, good and evil, mystery and clarity, but I am not filled with fear because I know the great Architect who is above and prior to them all. Nothing takes Him by surprise. Nothing in this universe is unknown and mysterious to Him, or undirected by Him. Even the presence of evils in the world that are a mystery to me do not cause me to despair, because I know that my wholly good and all-powerful God must have a morally sufficient reason for permitting them. Indeed, the very notion (categories) of good and evil would be meaningless and unintelligible were it not for an absolute God who takes evil seriously and provides the only adequate basis for objective moral judgments – impersonal atoms don't have a conscience! To posit evil presupposes an ultimate standard of good. Such a standard – to distinguish objectively between good and evil – is only provided for by the absolute God of Scripture. Crucially, in Jesus Christ, God does not stand at a distance, uninvolved, removed from evil and suffering, but in divine humility offers Himself to wicked and cruel people to die upon a Roman cross. Here, God turns evil intentions and works for His good purposes. In this sublime act of divine love, grace, and condescension God had a specific end in view, the recovery and redemption of this lost, marred and sinful world.

I also recognize that my "choice" and "freedom" to do good or evil only have meaning when rooted in the providence of God. For if chance is at the wheel of reality, then our "freedom" has no end (goal) in view, no teleological significance, and so this also is rendered meaningless – free to be and to do what? Freedom is not an end in itself! Freedom without God would be unintelligible because we would be in the bizarre position of our so-called freedom being fatalistically *determined* by impersonal chance. "Matter in motion" is not "free to choose" in any meaningful sense. Only as I see myself as being made in God's image, in relationship to His purposes, do my genuine choices have significance.

God is love. This God is concerned with every aspect of my life. I know that not a hair from my head nor a sparrow from the sky will fall without my God knowing and caring about it. In one of his psalms King David reminds us that God knows everything about us:

> O Lord, you have examined my heart
> And know everything about me.
> You know when I sit down or stand up.
> You know my every thought when far away.
> You chart the path ahead of me
> And tell me where to stop and rest.
> Every moment you know where I am.
> You know what I am going to say
> Even before I say it, Lord.
> You both precede and follow me.
> You place your hand of blessing on my head.
> Such knowledge is too wonderful for me,
> Too great for me to know.
> (Psalm 139:1-6)

Christ is higher than I and prior to me and I am content, therefore, to accept where there is mystery in God's activity in this world, for God is God and I am His creature, I am His Son. We do not share a common scale of being. He is the self-contained triune God, the infinite Creator; I am a finite creature. I occupy a finite realm of secondary causes in which I am able to choose freely whether I will serve the Creator or a creature. The omniscient God of the Bible is incomprehensible, occupying an infinite realm of ultimate causes where all of reality conforms to His exhaustive eternal plan.

To help us understand our relationship to God, consider childhood. Not all of us had positive experiences with our parents or of childhood as a whole, and sadly this can be an emotional barrier when we come to consider the being of God who reveals Himself as a father, but we can all put ourselves in the position of parents wanting the best for our children. I am grateful to God for the fact that my father is and was a man of faithfulness and integrity who loved his children. Yet he never told me all the reasons why he made certain decisions when I was a small child. For example, which town we would live in, which home we would buy, why I should go to school every day, be in church twice on Sundays, see the doctor when I felt perfectly well, brush my teeth twice a day, not play in the street in the evenings, or watch TV after 9 p.m. He offered little explanation for many things when I was very young. But I knew I could trust my parents and that was enough. Indeed, what was not explained to me was often for my own protection, for some burdens a child is not meant to carry.

Now, having children of my own, I realize the need to protect them by *not* explaining everything to them, or talking everything through with them when I make decisions. They are far too young and limited in experience, maturity, and knowledge at this stage, to understand why certain things are necessary. That is why children need parents. Life is about growth and development; maturation does not all happen in an instant. I realized, as a boy, that my mum and dad knew better than I about the world and its dangers and, though I complained at times and tested the boundaries, I realized they were there for my good even when I did not fully understand all of them.

My eldest daughter is just two and a half as I write this. She cannot survive in this world without faith. She must simply trust that mum and dad are present, trustworthy, and know what they are doing. All she need do is let out a cry! There is very little she can finally do for herself. She is not self-created, independent, self-determining and sustaining – she is as dependent as I am. I am also dependent on a relationship reflected in the one between myself and my daughter, I am dependent upon the Lord Jesus Christ, upon God my Father; I am as helpless as a newborn without Him, indeed every breath is His. My times are in His hands!

Of course, our human parents could never measure up to the moral perfection of God. I will fail as a father; I am fallible and will make mistakes. Thus, difficult as it may be, we should not project the failures of our parents onto God. His love and wisdom in dealing with His children are perfect. So I have no compulsion to fight my Father, the Father of lights, and Fountain of all knowledge and wisdom. I feel no need to struggle against the Lord Jesus Christ, my Master and Savior who said, "My purpose is to give life in all its fullness" (John 10:10).

Do I have questions like any child? Of course. Do I wrestle with my lack of understanding, frustrated by my inability to see the reasons behind all that God has permitted? Often! But that is the nature of our relationship; faith is a daily journey that is at times a real struggle. If there were no mystery, no struggle, no limitation or questions we would not need faith.

> [Faith] is the confident assurance that what we hope for is going to happen. It is the evidence of things we cannot yet see. (Hebrews 11:1)

Christ is the Creator, I am the creature. He is the parent, I am the child. He is infinite, immortal, invisible, and past finding out. I am finite, limited, weak, and ignorant. And yet I am made to reflect God's character, to grow increasingly in His likeness, to know and be known, to love Him and be loved. So the Scriptures say,

> ... to all who believed [Christ] and accepted him, he gave the right to become children of God. (John 1:12)

And,

> ... what manner of love the father has bestowed upon us, that we should be called children of God! (1 John 3:1 NKJV)

Infants seem so vulnerable, and they are! It is a vulnerable thing to acknowledge your utter dependence upon God. But my God is a good, just, and wise God, sending "rain on the just and the unjust" (Matthew 5:45) and filling our lives with good things even though we do not deserve them. I have seen what my God is like because He sent His only Son, the exact representation of His nature, into the world (see Hebrews 1:3). I choose therefore to trust Christ the Lord rather than finite, fallible, and fallen human beings (whoever they may be). When we come to understanding reality, what this world is, who we are, and how we may understand our relationship to God it is to Christ Jesus we must turn as a child looks to his or her father. As Cornelius Van Til has beautifully put it: "My unity is that of a child who walks with his father through the woods. The child is not afraid because its father knows it all and is capable of handling every situation."[4]

It is a hard but also liberating thing to recognize our weakness and dependence upon Christ for life and breath and all things. How many of us really want to acknowledge our profound limitations? How often are we prepared to admit that our doubts, fears, ignorance, and confusion are burdens we are tired of carrying? Why do we find it so hard to grant that our conscience has no peace and our minds no cognitive

---

4   From his pamphlet *Why I believe in God*.

rest when we realistically examine ourselves and our lives? But Jesus still invites us:

> Come to me, all of you who are weary and carry heavy burdens, and I will give you rest. Take my yoke upon you. Let me teach you, because I am humble and gentle, and you will find rest for your souls. (Matthew 11:28-29)

The autonomous person is a troubled soul, struggling to find rest and peace, thrown around in a sea of confusion. But when we come to Christ and *let Him teach us,* when our wisdom derives from Him, we find rest, because we find the unity, stability, and peace we seek in the authority of the person of Christ. Like drowning people hoisted aboard lifeboats we can cease to tread water, because we have found somewhere solid and stable to place our feet. I know of no other voice, no other call, no other source of authority, no other person in the entire history of civilization who can offer this unity – embodying unchanging truth, stability, peace, rest, and forgiveness of sin, substantiating those claims in life, death, and resurrection power. In Jesus Christ God has shown us not only our desperate need for redemption from moral corruption but also from intellectual foolishness. We need His rest but we will not receive it until we *learn from Him.* As God said through the prophet Isaiah:

> ... I will show that human wisdom is foolish and even the most brilliant people lack understanding. (Isaiah 29:14)

When the great and proud men of philosophy in century after century are reduced time and again to acknowledging the absurdity, vanity, and despairing futility of their own systems of thought, Christ stands alone in saying, "Let me teach you." In contrast, the great Scottish philosopher David Hume tells me I am nothing more than a "bundle of sense perceptions" and so nothing can be known with any certainty – not even the fact that I am a bundle! Friedrich Nietzsche admits that if there is no God we must even abandon the notion of grammar and thereby intelligible language – a doctrine that he followed with arguably admirable consistency, and which led to his own tragic personal insanity. Noted existentialist Jean-Paul Sartre tells me that I am a "bubble on the ocean of nothingness" and so we must simply look into the abyss and stare despair in the face. We are under no obligation to any ethical choice; good and evil collapse into one. In the lonely silence of existence, I must simply choose; it is the choice that matters, though why it matters, who can say? Consequently, even this "freedom" is rendered nonsense in the nothingness, free "choice" being "determined" by chance as I float about in the chaos. And the famous British philosopher and religious skeptic Bertrand Russell admits that his search for certainties has failed and that finally he cannot even justify his use of logic. All these autonomous, humanly conceived systems inevitably end here, in self-confessed ignorance and absurdity, refuting and undermining themselves. And so we hear the apostle Paul's rhetorical question echo down twenty centuries of history and philosophical thought:

> Where is the wise? Where is the scribe? Where is the disputer of this age? Has not God made foolish the wisdom of this world? (1 Corinthians 12:20 NKJV)

Firm Foundations

Define and explain these words and phrases:

1. Starting point
2. Syllogism

Answer the following questions:

1. What are some examples of non-believers "borrowing rocks" from the foundation of the Christian worldview? (p. 139-140)
2. The Christian unity of meaning shows up in cheerful and sorrowful times because it makes sense of and provides meaning to everything. Come up with a question based on this statement.
3. God often refers to Himself as a father. This can be difficult for some because human fathers are fallible, but that is to look at the issue backward. Rather, when we look at the God of the Bible, what do we learn about fatherhood?
4. Why does Joe say that 'freedom' in the abstract is not freedom at all? What is necessary for true freedom to exist?

CHAPTER 9

A MATTER OF THE HEART

"People who aren't Christians can't understand these truths from God's Spirit. It all sounds foolish to them because only those who have the Spirit can understand what the Spirit means. We who have the Spirit understand these things, but others can't understand us at all How could they? For,

'Who can know what the Lord is thinking?

Who can give him counsel?'

But we can understand these things, for we have the mind of Christ."

1 Corinthians 2:14-16

"You cried and called aloud, and broke my deafness. You flashed, shone and shattered my blindness. You breathed fragrance, I drew in my breath, and I pant for you. I tasted, I hunger and thirst. You touched me, and I burned for your peace."

- St. Augustine

BLIND GUIDES

It is very difficult to acknowledge that we may have been blind to the truth. I think this is particularly true of intellectuals and academics who so often pride themselves on their learning. Some people look for greatness in terms of political power or military greatness, others in sporting achievement or in the arts as celebrities. Some seek greatness purely in terms of wealth or influence and prestige, while others seek it in terms of learning and knowledge. Such people love to be recognized as "authorities." In my experience it is this latter group which is often most resistant to admitting blindness. Some of the intellectuals and academics of Jesus' day were known as Pharisees and were addressed by common people with the term "rabbi," meaning "teacher." In the gospels we read about how one day the first disciples pointed out to Jesus that some of these Pharisees were offended by His teaching; they were learned scholars who did not like to be corrected, especially by the "unschooled." Jesus said to His disciples:

> Every plant not planted by my heavenly Father will be rooted up, so ignore them. They are blind guides leading the blind, and if one blind person guides another, they will both fall into a ditch. (Matthew 15:13-14)

There are many blind guides and illegitimate "authorities" today who reject the Word of Christ, leading multitudes of people into all kinds of ditches. You find many such would-be gurus at every turn – for example, in the popular media, academic institutions, the political arena, and various non-Christian religious traditions – each pronouncing moral judgments and a rational independence in contradiction to the claims of Christ. Not all would do so consciously, of course, but it is endemic in the thinking of many. Ironically, despite the fact that the majority of the secular self-professed "experts" insist on philosophical uncertainty (skepticism), they are nonetheless certain that they are good guides. This makes their situation that much more serious.

In John 9 Christ deals directly with the intellectuals and scholars of His day who consider themselves good guides. In this passage Jesus has just healed a man born blind. The unbelieving Pharisees decide to interrogate this newly sighted, astonished individual because they are unwilling to accept that he had been born blind or that he had been healed by the man called Jesus. After the man's parents have been interrogated and have confirmed their son's blindness from birth, the Pharisees, now becoming agitated, demand to know exactly how Jesus had healed him. After hearing and rejecting the man's story, they call upon him to admit that Jesus *cannot be* the Son of God, for it is they who are the scholars and they are not aware of the origin of Jesus neither do they accept his authority! But the formerly blind man then argues that if Jesus were not from God, He could not have performed this unique healing. Whether they recognized His authority or not was irrelevant, He had demonstrated it through this miracle. Furious about being lectured by an ill-educated beggar upon religious and metaphysical matters they throw him out of the synagogue. John picks up the story as the man encounters Jesus again after his excommunication:

> When Jesus heard what had happened, he found the man and said, "Do you believe in the Son of Man?"
> The man answered, "Who is he, sir, because I would like to."
> "You have seen him," Jesus said, "and he is speaking to you!"
> "Yes, Lord," the man said, "I believe!" And he worshiped Jesus.
> Then Jesus told him, "I have come to judge the world. I have come to give sight to the blind and to show those who think they see that they are blind."
> The Pharisees who were standing there heard him and asked, 'Are you saying we are blind?'

"If you were blind, you wouldn't be guilty,' Jesus replied. "But you remain guilty because you claim you can see." (John 9:35-41)

What is Jesus suggesting here? What is the implication of His words? He is essentially attacking the claims of these learned scholars to authoritative insight; He exposes their blindness and illegitimate claim to true knowledge.

Few passages of Scripture identify so clearly the utter uniqueness of a truly Christian epistemology (view of knowledge). Jesus actually sets out the epistemological heart of His mission in the world. That mission is to bring true sight and understanding to those who will accept that they are spiritually blind and thereby intellectually hopelessly prejudiced, and to expose the blindness of those who think that they can see and understand without the revelation of the Son of God, the Word of truth.

THE LENS OF TRUTH

Cast your mind back to the analogy about my wife's spectacles. For most of the day she doesn't bother to wear them. But when she needs to drive somewhere, and so see where she is going, it is imperative that she puts them on; when she does, things become clear – cars as opposed to blurred shapes are moving down the road! On the other hand, I believe that I can see without her lenses. When I place my wife's glasses over my eyes, all becomes a blur, I am practically blinded, because I am slightly long-sighted whereas she is very short-sighted. So the clarity afforded an individual looking through a given set of spectacles actually depends on the initial condition of the eye: the lens remains the same.

Christ comes into the world to save human beings who are critically visually impaired, and thus like blind guides leading the blind. We have *all* been blinded by sin, through suppressing the truth, and are thereby alienated from God as a consequence; we are hopelessly placed to guide others by our own authority. Christ Jesus shows us, as the Creator and Sustainer of the world, that He is the *perfect lens* of interpretation. He alone is able to correct our marred vision. It is only through Him that we can see reality for what it really is.

The problem is that, like the Pharisees, many of us will not accept that we are visually impaired. In fact, unless God shows us by His Spirit that we are spiritually blind and consequently intellectually hostile to God, we will refuse to accept it. Here in John's gospel, Jesus tells these scholars that the greatest problem was not their blindness in itself: Christ the miracle maker is able to make the blind to see. The physical miracle He performed was a signpost pointing beyond itself to the greater miracle of opening the eyes of our understanding. He is able to do it, He is God the Son. So the most serious problem is not the blindness; it is the claim made by the blind to having perfect sight!

When Jesus asks the blind man, "Do you believe in the Son of Man?" (a title reserved for the Messiah, the Son of God), he actually confesses, "Yes, Lord, I believe!" and worships Him. He finds his unity at last in the worship of God whom he has now seen with his understanding, not just his physical eyes. He makes the one who gave him sight, Christ Jesus, his ultimate criterion for truth, rightly identifying Him as Lord over all, falling at His feet in worship! To this man, who acknowledged he could not see, a man prepared to obey the word of Christ (see John 9:7), Jesus gives sight and understanding. But to those who stood by convinced in their conceit that they could already see, rejecting His authority, Christ has something else to say. He shows them that if they had acknowledged their blindness they would not be guilty before God but already on the road to redemption and true knowledge through repentance and faith, expressing itself in worship, just as this beggar had worshiped Jesus. However, because they claim they can see, their guilt remains and the "lens of truth" in Christ serves only to blur the understanding, exposing their blindness to what is true (John 9:41). They remain blind guides, an awful and tragic condition.

It is Christ, then, who gives true sight both to the learned and the unlearned. We must all journey this same route. So it is hard for the intellectual, the academic, and the scholar to acknowledge they are as helpless as the potato picker in the realm of wisdom and true knowledge, regardless of qualifications or IQ. Sir Karl Popper, the twentieth-century British philosopher of science, wrote in his *Conjectures and refutations*, "Our knowledge can only be finite, while our ignorance must necessarily be infinite." The highly educated person who thinks at all, should arrive more quickly than most at the realization of their own ignorance. They simply know more about human ignorance than most! But Jesus was dealing with much more than our ignorance due to our finitude. It is not simply that we don't know enough and need additional knowledge or information. The problem is deeper than that. Rather, as we have seen, Jesus is teaching us that those without faith in Him are looking at reality the wrong way, through the wrong lens and with a wrong attitude.

Therefore, even what we do know we ultimately misinterpret. We have things turned up the wrong way and until we see them right side up, by seeing all things in the light of God's Word, we remain blind to the *true nature* of all things. This is why Blaise Pascal, one of Europe's greatest intellectuals, wrote these humbling words in the account of his conversion: "God of Abraham, God of Isaac, God of Jacob, not of philosophers and scholars." Why? Because He is the God of those who have faith, who do not attempt to de-throne God, taking Him at His word and submitting to His authority – He is the God of the humble. Pascal later wrote concerning the conversion to Christ of non-intellectuals: "Do not be surprised to find simple people believing without argument. For God makes them love him and hate themselves. He inclines their hearts to believe. We shall never believe with an effective belief and faith unless God inclines our heart."[1]

1 Pascal, *Mind on Fire*, 223.

A Matter of the Heart

The bottom line

The lens of truth found in Christ is unchanging. He claims to be the truth, the light of the world in whose rays all facts can be seen for what they are and through whom reality can be seen with utmost clarity. The question then remains, what kind of eyes do we need to see clearly through this lens? Why is it that some "eyes of the heart" perceive truth, whilst others miss it altogether? At what stage of development do the eyes of our understanding need to be in order for the truth to be everywhere plain to us?

Once a year I go to the optician for a check-up to ensure that my mild prescription does not need to be changed for a stronger pair of glasses. It is always a rather odd experience. Opticians do tend to invade your personal space as they get right in your face to peer into your eyes with a tiny light, looking for any new blemishes or problems. They then place a strange pair of heavy spectacles on your nose that have various slots in which they can slide round lenses. For the next ten minutes they chop and change them as you respond to questions about letters and colored lights on the illuminated box on the other side of the room. They generally begin by asking you to "read the bottom line" without the aid of the lenses. For me it is guesswork as I squint to try and read it. As I work my way up to the bigger letters on the lines above, things are a little easier. Then comes more chopping and changing, Better or worse, better or worse? until you can read the smallest letters. In the end there is only one set of lenses that will perfectly work for your eyes. Only one prescription will enable you to see things as they really are. Jesus claims to be the only lens through which reality can be seen, not for *some* but for *all* eyes. And here is the difference between physical and spiritual sight, between the physical eye and the eyes of our understanding. For our physical eyes we change the lenses to improve our sight; for understanding truth it is not the lens (Christ) but the "organ" itself that must adjust, for reality can be seen as it really is through only one lens!

Correcting the Eyes of the Heart

I can illustrate this once again by reflecting on physical eyesight. When I was a small boy of about six years of age I was having some difficulties at school with my handwriting. As I recall, each child was given a handwriting book in which you had to practice all the letters of the alphabet individually, keeping them between the top and bottom lines. I began to be consistently reprimanded by my teacher, Miss Daisly, for my scruffy and untidy handwriting. As I looked at my book, the letters, rather than staying in between the lines, would slowly progress diagonally across the page until the bottom of the letter barely touched the top line. I was deeply frustrated by this state of affairs because no matter how hard I tried, I couldn't get it right. Eventually my teacher spoke to my parents suspecting that it wasn't lazy, slovenly writing after all, perhaps I needed glasses. It turns out I did need glasses: I was significantly long-sighted. However, I was young enough for my vision to be corrected. By wearing these rather awful spectacles for about eighteen months, the muscles in my eyes strengthened and the eye settled down correctly. I could now take the glasses off and see with near-perfect vision. My eyes *themselves* (the organ) had been corrected by looking through a corrective lens. In my handwriting book I could finally keep my letters in the appropriate place.

In a similar way it is only a willing full exposure to the corrective lens of Christ and His revelation in the Scriptures that enables us to see clearly, correcting our marred perception. It is the eyes of our understanding that need to be adjusted. It is an interesting fact that when we get older our eyes can no longer be corrected in this way. Our eyes become set and will no longer adjust – like the hard hearts of the Pharisees who refused to be corrected in their conceit. There is something about childhood that makes us adjustable, malleable, teachable, and humble, both physically and mentally. We intuitively sense the profound limitation of our own understanding and it drives us to ask questions, inquire, and grow. Jesus often illustrated the sort of spiritual eyes needed to see the truth by speaking of little children. In fact, He likened the essential condition required to be able to see the truth to being childlike. A child is cognitively uniquely placed with a humble heart to be corrected and adjusted. Jesus, calling a small child over to Him, said to His disciples:

> I assure you, unless you turn from your sins and become as little children, you will never get into the Kingdom of Heaven. Therefore, anyone who becomes as humble as this little child is the greatest in the Kingdom of Heaven. (Matthew 18:3-4)

According to Christ, until our hearts are filled with appropriate humility, acknowledging our blindness and our spiritual and intellectual poverty, the deep assurance and certainty we seek will not be forthcoming. Despite being surrounded by God's self-revelation and although intellectually we are capable of following an argument revealing the futility of non-Christian thought, a rational proof does not become *personally persuasive* until the heart has been operated on. The rational proof of Christianity, showing the *impossibility of the contrary or transcendental necessity* of the triune God, in and of itself, does not move our will or change our moral desires! People can see and know truth all the time and yet suppress, distort, and turn away from it simply because it does not suit their preferences. Jesus demonstrated the rational necessity of belief in Him not least by His incredible miracles that modern empiricists claim would convert them should they see them today. But Christ's miracles did not simply effect a change in the will of multitudes that saw Him give sight to the blind, multiply loaves and fish, or even raise the dead – indeed, Christ knew full well that they did not do so. The haughty in heart were not persuaded even when Christ raised Lazarus from the grave after he had been dead for several days, the stench of decomposition in the air (John 11:40-48).

Rather, the Scriptures offer a particular route to personal certainty saying,

> God sets himself against the proud, But he shows favor to the humble. So humble yourselves under the mighty power of God, and in his good time he will honor you. (1 Peter 5:5-6)

If we are to know God's favor, comprehend reality and all of our life as it really is, we must cease to pretend that we can see when we are blind. Our hearts must be changed, our understanding must be adjusted; we must be converted.

IN CHRIST ALONE

We do love to imagine that we occupy *neutral ground* and make a decision when the evidence is in with respect to Christ's claims and His revelation. But the truth is that we have already placed our bet. We are already living and acting in a way that is either conducive or hostile to the knowledge of God. There is no neutral territory: either our eyes have been adjusted by the Spirit of God and the lens of biblical revelation, or they have not.

It becomes clear that Jesus teaches us that only those who submit to His revelation can see God, themselves, or the world for who and what they really are. It is foolish to suppose that God will randomly offer dramatic proofs, as demanded by some, to people who taunt, tempt, and mock Him, to those who merely seek a sign. Jesus called people who presumptuously demand signs *"evil and faithless"* (Matthew 16:4). God has chosen uniquely to manifest Himself in *Christ alone,* His miraculous life, substitutionary death upon the cross for our forgiveness, and His bodily resurrection. That is the historical sign He has given: He has given us His Son and His Word which by the Holy Spirit of wisdom and revelation rightly interprets the world. Pascal incisively sums up the proof God offers:

> Jesus Christ is the only proof of the living God. We only know God through Jesus Christ. Without his mediation there is no communication with God. But through Jesus Christ we know God. All who have claimed to know God and to prove his existence without Jesus Christ have done so ineffectively . . . In [Christ] and through him, we know God. Apart from him, and without scripture, without original sin, without the necessary mediator who was promised and who came, it is impossible to prove absolutely that God exists, or to teach sound doctrine and sound morality. But through and in Jesus Christ we can prove God's existence, and teach both doctrine and morality. Jesus Christ therefore is the true God of me.[2]

Pascal is emphasizing that it is in Jesus Christ alone that we have the proof of God and knowledge of God. It is by starting with Christ revealed in Scripture that we arrive at the truth and proof we seek. As we presuppose the truth of His self-revelation we see the folly of so-called "human wisdom" and also the futility of trying to prove God outside of His revelation in Christ.

Likewise the apostle Paul writes in the New Testament:

> Since God in his wisdom saw to it that the world would never find him through human wisdom, he has used our foolish preaching to save all who believe. God's way seems foolish to the Jews because they want a sign from heaven to prove that it is true. And it is foolish to the Greeks because they believe only what agrees with their own wisdom. So when we preach

---

2 *Ibid.*, 147.

> that Christ was crucified, the Jews are offended, and
> the Gentiles say it's all nonsense. But to those called
> by God to salvation, both Jews and Gentiles, Christ is
> the mighty power of God and the wonderful wisdom
> of God. This 'foolish' plan of God is far wiser than
> the wisest of human plans, and God's weakness is far
> stronger than the greatest of human strength.
> (1 Corinthians 1:21-25)

So my argument in this book has not been intended to impress you or persuade you that with *my wisdom* I have worked all things out and come to know truth through human ingenuity, but rather that everything, *"all the treasures of wisdom and knowledge,"* as Paul the apostle writes (Colossians 2:3), are found *in Christ.* Everything is dependent upon Him, the Alpha and Omega, the beginning and the end! I have sought to show, finally, that without Christ all human thinking and endeavor is reduced to folly and absurdity. And I affirm that God *has* provided visible verification of His character and intentions through the incarnation of the Lord Jesus Christ, in real space-time history!

The gift of God

All of this leads us to understand that we cannot know God as we should or understand His revelation properly without standing in appropriate relationship to God. And Christ tells us that the only way this can happen is by humbling ourselves. We must repent of our sin and trust Christ for deliverance from the righteous wrath of God. We must put our faith in Him and His death on the cross, where he voluntarily paid the just penalty for sin for those who will believe. It is in this act of repentance, which involves a "change of mind," that we draw near to God and are put right with God. As we do this, the Bible teaches, He will correspondingly draw near to us in His manifest presence, filling us with His immeasurable love and grace and revealing His full salvation. The apostle Paul identifies this wonderful work of God for us when He writes:

> Now we have received, not the spirit of the world, but the Spirit who is from God, that we might know the things that have been freely given to us by God. (1 Corinthians 2:12 NKJV)

It is then that we enter into a new quality of life and *knowledge* as our entire being undergoes epistemic reorientation and our minds and hearts are united with Christ. This, ultimately, is why I believe. I have the testimony of the Holy Spirit in my understanding that I belong to God. Scripture tells us that,

> . . . his Holy Spirit speaks to us deep in our hearts and tells us that we are God's children. (Romans 8:16)

We can know God as our own dear Father (Romans 8:15). Jesus describes what leads to this experience as being "born again." So we see that the true Christian possesses a certainty that includes yet supersedes mere intellectual affirmation. My life of faith is no more a mere intellectual matter than my marriage is. It involves a willingness to commit to personal communion, a filial relationship of passionate commitment. It is through such a relationship that the overwhelming assurance of the reality and presence of God in our lives arises. I can no more know God as a mere object for study than I know my wife or children as objects of study. I know them because I relate to them intimately. This highlights the essentially relational nature of true knowledge, also making clear that it is the infinitely relational triune God in gracious condescension who takes the initiative in drawing us into relationship with Himself. The Bible affirms this truth that Christ Jesus came to seek and to save the lost (Luke 19:10).

    The faith that I have as a Christian, the reason I still believe in Jesus, is because God has given me the *gift of faith*. This is not because I deserve it or because my life in some way warrants such a gift. Indeed, we have here something of a high paradox. God requires faith from us and yet, because our willful rebellious hearts refuse to come in faith, He must grant us the grace to put our faith in Him. But remember there is no contradiction here when we maintain the Creator/creature distinction – we live in this world of secondary causes and do not share a common scale of being with God, the God of primary and ultimate causes. As individual persons possessed of a will, we must act fully, with our entire being, and choose to trust Christ; we have no valid excuse for rejecting or disobeying Him. Yet as we are dependent beings, God must act fully also, in His sovereign providence. Never are our wills most truly human, most truly our own, as when they are willingly and increasingly surrendered with joy to the will of God.

So, because of the gift of faith, I can see what many others cannot see, not because I am in any way superior or any more humble in and of myself than others, but because God by His grace *inclined my heart* to believe. He is the all-conditioning one. He has shaped, molded, and taught me from childhood and throughout my adult life to believe in His Son. Pascal wrote of this same gift of faith and conditioning:

> Faith is a gift of God. So do not imagine that it can be described as a gift of reason . . . this is the faith God himself puts into our hearts, although *he often uses proof as the instrument.* 'Faith comes from hearing the message' (Romans 10 v 17). But this faith dwells in our hearts, and helps us to say not 'I know', but 'I believe.'[3]

It is that belief, that faith (more than intellectual affirmation), which has opened my understanding, and many times in my life God has used proof as the instrument of strengthening and encouraging me. My faith has "sought understanding" and has led me to see that without this faith there could be no understanding of anything or proof of any kind. He has also used

---

3   *Ibid.*

proof through me as an instrument to lead others to Christ and I have always considered it a privilege that God would use someone like me to be involved in His wonderful sovereign work. Perhaps the proofs I have offered in this account of my belief, God will use, in His kindness, to open your eyes also and put faith into your heart.

At this point you might well be asking yourself why, to your knowledge, you were not inclined to believe during your childhood, or why as yet you have not been given this gift. Is God unjust or unfair? Does God's activity exhibit a random partiality? Not at all. In our hearts we know full well that God is not unfair; in fact, the idea of fairness has no meaning without Him. If we are honest, we are all conscious deep down that God has not left us in the dark with respect to His being and nature. He certainly does not incline all hearts in *exactly the same way*, but He provides adequate testimony of Himself in every place and in every heart universally, for all time. The psalmist writes in Psalm 19:1-4:

> The heavens tell of the glory of God.
> The skies display his marvelous craftsmanship.
> Day after day they continue to speak;
> Night after night they make him known.
> They speak without a sound or a word;
> Their voice is silent in the skies;
> Yet their message has gone out to all the earth,
> And their words to all the world.

The apostle Paul also tells us that God has revealed sufficient of Himself in the wonder of creation (including our use of reason and of logic, in our moral awareness, our sense of beauty and human dignity, and use of our will) to render us without any excuse for not coming to Him in humility (see Romans 1:18-23). When we all stand before God at the judgment, there will be no person who will be able to say in truth that they wanted to come to God in faith, but He did not enable them – such a person does not exist. Those who reject Christ as the Creator and Redeemer of this world have willfully chosen to do so. Multitudes of men and women have hated God to His face. I have spoken with people who have told me that they do not care what God requires or what He will do or say, claiming they would challenge God to His face, and I have heard people make blasphemous challenges to God – they too have chosen this path of hostility to God. On the other hand, those who are accepted by God because of faith are people who have chosen to live in faithfulness to the call of the gospel.

Furthermore, the gospel is a universal invitation from which no one is excluded. There is no class of sins, no people group, no demographic which leads to exclusion from the call of the gospel. John Calvin, in the *Institutes of the Christian Religion*, writes: "[God] calls all men to himself, without a single exception, and gives Christ to all, that we might be illumined by him." And again, in his commentary on the book of Acts, Calvin writes: "As no-man is excluded from calling upon God, the gate of salvation is set open to all men; neither is there any other thing which keepeth us back from entering in, save only our own unbelief."[4]

The very fact that you have endured my argument thus far and not torn up this book and tossed it in the fire, is itself an indication that my wonderful gracious Father is inclining your heart to see the truth and meet the Savior, that He may be my God and your God, my Savior and your Savior.

---

4   John Calvin. *Commentary upon the Acts of the Apostles*. Translated and edited by Henry Beveridge. Grand Rapids: Christian Classics Ethereal Library, n.d. https://ccel.org/ccel/calvin/calcom36/calcom36.ix.iii.html?queryID=7985694&resultID=120003.

A Matter of the Heart

Define and explain these words and phrases:

1. Epistemology
2. Repentance

Answer the following questions:

1. Summarize the eyeglasses analogy. (p. 158-159)
2. Why does Joe describe faith as a paradox? How is this paradox resolved? Do you find this explanation compelling? How would you explain faith in the Christian worldview?
3. Have you heard the argument before that God must be unjust to give saving faith to some and not others? How would you respond?

Chapter 10
The Robin and the Egg

"Therefore if any man be in Christ, he is a new creature: old things are passed away; behold, all things are become new."

2 Corinthians 5:17 KJV

"New birth means surrendering ourselves back to God in Christ, after which we will have a life which is absolutely supernatural, not created but begotten [of the father]."

- C. S. Lewis

After birth

Scripture teaches us there is no other route to discovering God or the true treasures of wisdom and knowledge; only through this new birth of which Jesus speaks can these infinite riches be found. Jesus gave us no other choice. He said, "I assure you, unless you are born again, you can never see the Kingdom of God" (John 3:3).

Reflecting on this I am reminded that recently a robin made her nest on top of one of the columns supporting our porch at the front of our home in Ontario, Canada. We watched her for several weeks as she sat on her eggs. One evening, we finally noticed three mouths gaping open, waiting to be fed, and mum hurrying backwards and forwards with worms and insects. At night she would sit as a protective mother warming those infant robins. Imagine a chick inside one of those eggs close to hatching time. Imagine you could talk and reason with that chick. Imagine trying to persuade the chick that outside the world of its shell was a great wide world with all the wonders of creation waiting to be discovered or that its loving mother was patiently waiting for it to hatch. Imagine trying to convince the chick that the interior of its shell was not the world, just an infinitely small part of it. Even if it could think and reason like a human being it could neither fully understand nor accept any of the arguments you presented, no matter how powerful your logic: you could never coerce belief. The chick has to hatch. It must be born again into the world outside the shell where the evidence is seen for what it is – inescapable and overwhelming.

Given that we ourselves weave a cocoon, a shell of sin, around us, shielding us from reality in our hostility to God, we suffer from a similar form of epistemological myopia. So I acknowledge again at the close of my argument that I do not pretend to have proved to you that you need to be born again, but I hope I have challenged you to consider that it is necessary for you to be born again. The Lord Jesus Himself commands that you must be and Scripture invites you to "taste and see that the Lord is good" (Psalm 34:8).

Part of the Plan

I hope I have been able to show in the previous pages that the degree to which any human being will finally come to know God as Father is directly related to the degree to which we are graciously brought to see, and are willing to participate in, *God's plan of salvation* and reconciliation. The difficulty for people knowing God and seeing the truth of Christian theism is *not* then due to a lack of evidence or because of the "great reach" of the non-believers' intellect compared to those often labeled naïve Christians. Rather, it is because people willfully resist participating in this plan and so suppress and set aside God's clear revelation, resulting in a darkened understanding and a refusal to humble themselves due to an ethical hostility to God. True understanding is simply impossible whilst we reject God's self-authenticating revelation to us in Scripture. Just as we need to assume the reliability of the human eye to confirm the reliability of the human eye – because that is just the nature of physical sight – so we need to presuppose the reliability of Scripture if we want to evaluate the teaching of Scripture rationally; even those who would attempt to deny its reliability, must *borrow* its truths to form an argument because that is just the nature of real knowledge! We must literally assume the truth of the Word in order to examine the Word and the world of which it speaks rationally. In this God's revelation is shown to be inescapably true! Is this circular? All argument has a necessarily circular character, but this circle alone shows itself to be the only possible sound foundation for thinking and knowing (it is not a flat circle). Creation itself is a revelation of God and this revelation is unintelligible without accepting the authority of God's written revelation to interpret it!

I do not presume that my argument is easy to accept;

in fact, it is entirely unacceptable to the would-be autonomous person with spiritual cataracts over their eyes. Neither do I claim to have removed all difficulties in this short book, I simply cannot do that. But this message can be tested by the sincere heart seeking after God; it can be verified not just rationally, but in the immediacy of our personal experience if we will be obedient to the voice of Christ.

Neither the Kingdom of God, nor the truth concerning Jesus can be arrived at through a pretended *independent, self-governing* human reasoning. Even a correct application of the laws of logic does not inescapably lead to the truth as if we can *supply* and are neutral in our assessment of "facts." As we have seen, such a neutrality assumes that both logic and facts of experience can operate over and above or independent of God. Various noted rationalists (i.e. Spinoza, Descartes, Leibniz) who all claimed to be applying a pure logic and reason to "reality" arrived at different accounts of reality. This shows that you can take rules of thought and apply them to almost any *starting point* and come up with a philosophy that is at least internally consistent (valid), even if based on outlandish premises (unsound) that nobody else could accept, premises like "all the world is insane except for me." Merely adding tests like "empirical adequacy" doesn't help either, because sense experience is interpreted in the light of our presuppositions. For example, the madman who believes himself to be dead, on seeing his own blood flow out, will simply affirm that dead men bleed after all. It is only when the epistemological foundations are examined that we see the folly of unbelieving thought. We have seen that logic itself only has rational warrant where God is presupposed. Christianity alone provides the pre-conditions necessary for the intelligible experience.

THE WISE, THE CLEVER, AND THE CHILDLIKE

Nothing could more effectively summarize the biblical view of the knowledge of God presented in my argument than Jesus' profound words in Matthew's gospel:

> O Father, Lord of heaven and earth, thank you for hiding the truth from those who think themselves so wise and clever, and for revealing it to the childlike. Yes, Father, it pleased you to do it this way! My Father has given me authority over everything. No one really knows the Son except the Father, and no one really knows the Father except the Son and those to whom the Son chooses to reveal him. (Matthew 11:25-27)

It is Jesus Himself who gives direct testimony of His life, presence, character, and nature when His saving revelation comes to a humble childlike heart, regenerated by the Holy Spirit. In the Word of God and this world He has made, all the evidence one could ever desire is given to that person willing to see it; to the one who humbles his or her entire being – heart, mind, soul, and strength before the God and Father of the Lord Jesus Christ.

Are you, am I, entitled to know God? Are we worthy of knowing God? The truth is that we know we are not worthy. Thus, if we are to have this unspeakable gift, on what ground other than that stipulated by God Himself in Christ, a God who loves us and calls us to seek Him while He may be found – a personal, holy, and righteous Father who promises He will be found by us as we draw near to Him (James 4:8)?

I was one of those infants that Christ speaks of in Matthew 11, just a young boy when Christ took hold of my life. But even at that tender age I was conscious of God's revelation and so of my sin, my failure, my inherent need for God. I have been conscious of my heart's tendency for rebellion as I war with the "old man" (sinful desires) and yet also Christ's striving with me to preserve me in all my foolish attempts to assert an illusory independence. I am conscious that, had He not been with me all those years according to the promises of His covenant and revealed the Father to me by His good pleasure, I would be utterly lost. Christ has saved me from sin because He has saved me from myself – not because I welcomed Him or was wise enough to embrace the truth but because He inclined my heart. As the psalmist prayed in Psalm 119:36 (NKJV), "Incline my heart to Your testimonies, and not to covetousness."

I still believe in Jesus because He has loved me with an everlasting love, delivering me from my own foolish inclinations and futile thoughts. A futility that leads many human beings to hold that the egg could have come before the robin! That humanity is original and prior to any god we may have invented in our minds. A folly that leads rebels to ignore the reality that without God, the Father of creation, there could be no human experience to speak of, something plainly taught to my little girl by the robin who first needed to lay her eggs in the nest before they could hatch.

Jesus Christ, the eternal Word, the Creator and Redeemer of humanity, is the very pre-condition[1] of rational thought, reason, and logic. Without Him there could be no objective moral value judgements, no distinction between moral beauty and ugliness, no intrinsic human dignity, and no meaningful choice. Without Him there is no foundation for human language or intelligible argument, or for the uniformity in nature or practical apparatus of science; in fact, there is no foundation for any human knowledge. Without Him all assumed cause and effect relationships are unintelligible. In fact, without Christ, nothing can be said at all, we cannot meaningfully communicate, my writing this book and your reading it would be impossible – He is the pre-condition of it all. Without Him, all distinctions collapse into an indistinguishable blank nothingness making rationality impossible, or we drown in a sea of matter in motion, neither unified nor differentiated, where human experience is rendered absurd in the meaningless void of chance. Christ alone makes sense of it all, and that is *why I still believe in Jesus*. He is the eternal

---

1   Put philosophically, Christ (the triune Godhead) is a transcendental necessity for human experience to be intelligible. The Christian world view alone can account for the intelligibility of our experience.

Word (the *logos* thought and logic of God), the foundation of all being, the pre-condition of it all. We are His image and the world everywhere bears His imprint! Nothing could be but by the finger of the triune God and in sublime mystery the eternal Word, the second person of the Godhead, became flesh, a human being, taking a fingerprint all of His own and lived among us. In Him God's identity, His image, is manifest and in Him our true identity is revealed.

Outside the egg, I can see all this. I am not a prisoner of the shell of sin; I have hatched into a new view of reality. Like a caterpillar escaping the chrysalis it had made for itself discovers a new view of life, the perspective of a butterfly, I have undergone a total transformation, as has every true Christian.

Critical choices

Having heard all that has been said about Christ and His way of salvation it is crucial that we respond in an appropriate way. Radical truth calls for radical change. News of seismic proportions should cause a seismic reaction in our thoughts and actions. The reality of our blindness through sin calls us to prayer for new sight. To assume that all we have seen is a mere intellectual matter of passing interest, requiring no response on our part would be a terrible mistake. This is not something that we can leave to our leisure like a choice of a new car or career. It is a rational necessity, a moral imperative and, most importantly, a divine command of eternal significance. I would be failing the reader and my Lord and Savior were I not to spell out the consequences of continuing pretended neutrality, indifference, and rejection of the call of Christ. John Calvin sums the biblical message up appropriately when he writes in the *Institutes*, "After the impious [rebellious] have willfully shut their own eyes, it is the righteous vengeance of God upon them to darken their understandings, so that, seeing, they may not perceive."

This is a terrible judgment to befall anyone, that they should be granted their own will in shutting their eyes to the truth (being conscious of God's revelation), and so invite upon themselves the judgement of God whereby He allows the understanding to become darkened in its own conceit leaving that person hopelessly blind to the truth about themselves, God, and the world. This fatal blindness leads eventually to an eternal separation from the life and presence of God in the darkness of our own ignorance and moral corruption – a place where hostility to God grows ever more potent, a place the Bible calls Hell. Here, Jesus says, "There will be weeping and gnashing of teeth" (Matthew 8:12). This clearly indicates that Hell is a place of sorrow, misery, and teeth-grinding anger and hostility to God and others.

I appeal to you to avoid this course at all costs and embrace instead the wonderful invitation of the Bible. The Scriptures say,

> . . . Today is the day of salvation. (2 Corinthians 6:2)

> O that you would listen to his voice today. (Psalm 95:7)

The apostle Paul writes in Romans 10:8-11:

> Salvation that comes from trusting Christ – which is the message we preach – is already within easy reach. In fact, the Scriptures say, 'The message is close at hand; it is on your lips and in your heart.' For if you confess with your mouth that Jesus is Lord and believe in your heart that God raised him from the dead, you will be saved. For it is by believing in your heart that you are made right with God, and it is by confessing with your mouth that you are saved. As the Scriptures tell us, 'Anyone who believes in him will not be disappointed.'

Jesus Himself calls us to come to Him and assures us, "the one who comes to Me I will by no means cast out" (John 3:37 NKJV). Each of us can call upon God. We can cry out to God for new sight, for rescue and mercy, for life and salvation, for forgiveness, for the light of truth to break into our lives no matter how dark they may be, for Jesus Christ has said with regard to salvation, "with God everything is possible" (Matthew 19:26). He assures us, "you will know the truth, and the truth will set you free" (John 8:32).

The prayer of the hymn writer seems especially relevant for those earnestly seeking Him, a prayer that we can offer up to God:

> Pass me not, O gentle Savior
> Hear my humble cry
> While on other thou art smiling
> Do not pass me by.
>
> Let me at a throne of mercy
> Find a sweet release
> Kneeling there in deep contrition
> Help my unbelief.
>
> Savior, Savior
> Hear my humble cry
> While on others thou art calling
> Do no pass me by.[2]

It was as Jesus was passing along a road out of Jericho that He heard the cries of a blind man named Bartimaeus calling out, "Son of David, have mercy on me" (see Mark 10:46-52). Jesus commanded that he be brought to Him. His disciples, having at first told the man to be quiet, said to blind Bartimaeus, "Cheer up . . . he's calling you." Having stood up and come forward, Jesus approached the man and asked him a simple

---

2   "Pass Me Not, O Gentle Savior" by Fanny J. Crosby (1820-1915).

question, "What do you want me to do for you?" The blind man responded, "Teacher, I want to see." Jesus said to him, "Your faith has healed you." And instantly he received his sight!

If you will look with the eyes and listen with the ears of your heart, you will see that Christ is standing close by and speaking to you! Take courage, venture to cry out to Jesus in faith and sincerity of heart and He will hear you and call you forth, granting you true sight, light, truth, and new life, both now and for all eternity.

> He who has ears to hear, let him hear!
> (Matthew 11:15 NKJV)

The Robin and the Egg

Define and explain these words and phrases:

1. Pre-condition
2. Rationalism

Answer the following questions:

1. Joe raises the question of circularity in logic. Is there a valid kind of circular reasoning? How would you distinguish between valid and invalid circularity?
2. Explain why Joe claims that Jesus Christ is the necessary pre-condition for rational thought, reason and logic. What is it about Christ that makes it so? Could anything or anyone else suffice as this pre-condition?

www.ingramcontent.com/pod-product-compliance
Lightning Source LLC
Chambersburg PA
CBHW021442070526
44577CB00002B/259